C Programming Lan

Praveen Shandilya

**Preface** i

**Contents** ii

**Chapter 1**

## Introduction

This textbook was written with two primary objectives. The first is to introduce the C programming language. C is a practical and still-current software tool; it remains one of the most popular programming languages in existence, particularly in areas such as embedded systems. C facilitates writing code that is very efficient and powerful and, given the ubiquity of C compilers, can be easily ported to many different platforms. Also, there is an enormous code-base of C programs developed over the last 30 years, and many systems that will need to be maintained and extended for many years to come.

The second key objective is to introduce the basic concepts of software design. At one-level this is C-specific: to learn to design, code and debug complete C programs. At another level, it is more general: to learn the necessary skills to design large and complex software systems. This involves learning to decompose large problems into manageable systems of modules; to use modularity and clean interfaces to design for correctness, clarity and flexibility.

### 1.    Programming and Programming Languages

The native language of a computer is binary—ones and zeros—and all instructions and data must be provided to it in this form. Native binary code is called *machine* language. The earliest digital electronic computers were programmed directly in binary, typically via punched cards, plug-boards, or front-panel switches. Later, with the advent of terminals with keyboards and monitors, such programs were written as sequences of hexadecimal numbers, where each hexadecimal digit represents a four binary digit sequence. Developing correct programs in machine language is tedious and complex, and practical only for very small programs.

In order to express operations more abstractly, *assembly* languages were developed. These languages have simple mnemonic instructions that directly map to a sequence of machine language operations. For example, the MOV instruction moves data into a register, the ADD instruction adds the contents of two registers together. Programs written in assembly language are translated to machine code using an *assembler* program. While assembly languages are a considerable improvement on raw binary, they still very low-level and unsuited to large-scale programming. Furthermore, since each processor provides its own assembler dialect, assembly language programs tend to be non-portable; a program must be rewritten to run on a different machine.

The 1950s and 60s saw the introduction of high-level languages, such as Fortran and Algol. These languages provide mechanisms, such as subroutines and conditional looping constructs, which greatly enhance the structure of a program, making it easier to express the progression of instruction execution; that is, easier to visualise program flow. Also, these mechanisms are an abstraction of the underlying machine instructions and, unlike assembler, are not tied to any particular hardware. Thus, ideally, a program written in a high-level language may be ported to a different machine and run without change. To produce executable code from such a program, it is translated to machine- specific assembler language by a *compiler* program, which is then coverted to machine code by an assembler (see Appendix B for details on the compilation process).

Compiled code is not the only way to execute a high-level program. An alternative is to translate the program on-the-fly using an *interpreter* program (e.g., Matlab, Python, etc). Given a text-file containing a high-level program, the interpreter reads a high-level instruction and then executes the necessary set of low-level operations. While usually slower than a compiled program, interpreted code avoids the overhead of compilation-time and so is good for rapid implementation and testing. Another alternative, intermediate between compiled and interpreted code, is provided by a *virtual machine* (e.g., the Java virtual machine), which behaves as an abstract-machine layer on top of a real machine. A high-level program is compiled to a special *byte-code* rather than machine language, and this intermediate code is then interpreted by the virtual machine program. Interpreting byte code is usually much faster than interpreting high-level code directly. Each of these representations has is relative advantages: compiled code is typically fastest, interpreted code is highly portable and quick to implement and test, and a virtual machine offers a combination of speed and portability.

The primary purpose of a high-level language is to permit more direct expression of a programmer's design. The algorithmic structure of a program is more apparent, as is the flow of information between different program components. High-level code modules can be designed to "plug" together piece-by-piece, allowing large programs to be built out of small, comprehensible parts. It is important to realise that programming in a high-level language is about communicating a software design to programmers *not* to the computer. Thus, a programmer's focus should be on modularity and readability rather than speed. Making the program run fast is (mostly) the compiler's concern.

1.    **The C Programming Language**

C is a general-purpose programming language, and is used for writing programs in many different domains, such as operating systems, numerical computing, graphical applications, etc. It is a small language, with just 32 keywords (see [HS95, page 23]). It provides "high-level" structured- programming constructs such as statement grouping, decision making, and looping, as well as "low- level" capabilities such as the ability to manipulate bytes and addresses.

> *Since C is relatively small, it can be described in a small space, and learned quickly. A programmer can reasonably expect to know and understand and indeed regularly use the entire language [KR88, page 2].*

C achieves its compact size by providing spartan services within the language proper, foregoing many of the higher-level features commonly built-in to other languages. For example, C provides no operations to deal directly with composite objects such as lists or arrays. There are no memory management facilities apart from static definition and stack-allocation of local variables. And there are no input/output facilities, such as for printing to the screen or writing to a file.

Much of the functionality of C is provided by way of software routines called *functions*.

The language is accompanied by a *standard library* of functions that provide a collection of commonly- used operations. For example, the standard function printf() prints text to the screen (or, more precisely, to *standard output*—which is typically the screen). The standard library will be used extensively throughout this text; it is important to avoid writing your own code when a correct and portable implementation already exists.

### 1. A First Program

> *A C program, whatever its size, consists of* functions *and* variables. *A function contains* statements *that specify the computing operations to be done, and variables store values used during the computation [KR88, page 6].*

The following program is the traditional first program presented in introductory C courses and textbooks.

```
1. /* First C program: Hello World */
2. #include <stdio.h>
3
```
```
1. int main(void)
2. {
3.      printf("Hello World!\n");
4. }
```

5. Comments in C start with /* and are terminated with */. They can span multiple lines and are not nestable. For example,

> /* this attempt to nest two comments /* results in just one comment, ending here: */ and the remaining text is a syntax error. */

1. Inclusion of a standard library header-file. Most of C's functionality comes from libraries. Header- files contain the information necessary to use these libraries, such as function declarations and macros.

2. All C programs have main() as the entry-point function. This function comes in two forms:

> int main(void)
> int main(int argc, char *argv[])

The first takes no arguments, and the second receives command-line arguments from the environment in which the program was executed—typically a command-shell. (More on command-line arguments in Section 13.4.) The function returns a value of type int (i.e., an *integer*).

1. and 7 The braces { and } delineate the extent of the function block. When a function completes, the program returns to the calling function. In the case of main(), the program terminates and control returns to the environment in which the program was executed. The integer return value of main() indicates the program's exit status to the environment, with 0 meaning normal termination.

2. This program contains just one statement: a function call to the standard library function printf(), which prints a *character string* to standard output (usually the screen). Note, printf() is not a part of the C language, but a function provided by the standard library (declared in header stdio.h). The standard library is a set of functions mandated to exist on all systems conforming to the ISO C standard. In this case, the printf() function takes one *argument* (or input parameter): the *string*

_constant_ "Hello World!\n". The \n at the end of the string is an _escape character_ to start a new line. Escape characters provide a mechanism for representing hard-to-type or invisible characters (e.g., \t for tab, \b for backspace, \" for double quotes). Finally, the statement is terminated with a semicolon (;). C is a free-form language, with program meaning unaffected by whitespace in most circumstances. Thus, statements are terminated by ; not by a new line.

## 3.  **Variants of Hello World**

The following program produces identical output to the previous example. It shows that a new line is not automatic with each call to printf(), and subsequent strings are simply abutted together until a \n escape character occurs.

```
1. /* Hello World version 2 */
2. #include <stdio.h>
3
1. int main(void)
2. {
3.      printf("Hello ");
4.      printf ("World!");
5.      printf ("\n");
6. }
```

The next program also prints "Hello World!" but, rather than printing the whole string in one go, it prints it one character at a time. This serves to demonstrate several new concepts, namely: types, variables, identifiers, pointers, arrays, array subscripts, the \0 (NUL) escape character, logical operators, increment operators, while-loops, and string formatting.

This may seem a lot, but don't worry—you don't have to understand it all now, and all will be explained in subsequent chapters. For now, suffice to understand the basic structure of the code: a string, a loop, an index parameter, and a print statement.

```
1. /* Hello World version 3 */
2. #include <stdio.h>
3
1. int main(void)
5{
1.      int i = 0;
2.      char *str= "HelloWorld!\n";
8
1.      /* Print each character until reach \0 ' */
2.      while (str[i]  !=  '\0')
3.          printf("%c", str[i++]);
12
1.      return 0;
2. }
```

13 Unlike the previous versions of this program, this one includes an explicit return statement for the program's exit status.

**Style note.** Throughout this text take notice of the formatting style used in the example code, particularly indentation. Indentation is a critical component in writing clear C programs. The compiler does not care about indentation, but it makes the program easier to read for programmers.

*1.* **A Numerical Example**


2. /* Fahrenheit to Celcius conversion table (K&R page 12) */
3. #include <stdio.h>

3
1. int main(void)
2. {
3.      float fahr, celsius;
4.      int lower, upper, step;

8
9      /* Set lower and upper limits of the temperature table (in Fahrenheit) along with the
1.      * table increment step-size */
2.      lower = 0;
3.      upper = 300;
4.      step = 20;

14
1.      /* Create conversion table using the equation: C = (5/9)(F - 32) */
2.      fahr = lower;
3.          while     (fahr <=   upper) {
4.          celsius = (5.0/9.0) * (fahr-32.0);
5.          printf("°/,3.0f \t°/,6.1f\n", fahr, celsius);
6.          fahr += step;
7.      }
8. }


₆₋₇ This program uses several *variables*. These must be declared at the top of a block, before any statements. Variables are specified *types*, which are int and float in this example.

₉₋₁₀ Note, the * beginning line 10 is not required and is there for purely aesthetic reasons.

1.     ₁₃ These first three statements in the program initialise the three integer variables.

₁₆ The floating-point variable fahr is initialised. Notice that the two variables are of different type (int and float). The compiler performs automatic type *conversion* for compatible types.

₁₇₋₂₁ The while-loop executes while ever the expression (fahr <= upper) is TRUE. The operator <= means LESS THAN OR EQUAL TO. This loop executes a *compound statement* enclosed in braces— these are the three statements on lines 18-20.

1. This statement performs the actual numerical computations for the conversion and stores the result in the variable celcius.

2. The printf() statement here consists of a format string and two variables fahr and celcius. The format string has two *conversion specifiers*, %3.0f and %6.1f, and two escape characters, tab and new-line. (The conversion specifier %6.1f, for example, formats a floating-point number allowing space for at least six digits and printing one digit after the decimal point. See Section 13.1.1 for more information on printf() and conversion specifiers.)

3. The assignment operator += produces an expression equivalent to fahr = fahr + step.
   **Style note.** Comments should be used to clarify the code where necessary. They

should explain intent and point-out algorithm subtleties. They should avoid restating code idioms. Careful choice of identifiers (i.e., variable names, etc) can greatly reduce the number of comments required to produce readable code.

## 1.　Another Version of the Conversion Table Example

This variant of the conversion table example produces identical output to the first, but serves to introduce symbolic constants and the for-loop.

```
1. /* Fahrenheit to Celcius conversion table (K&R page 15) */
2. #include <stdio.h>
3
1. #define LOWER 0/* lower limit of temp. table (in Fahrenheit) */
2. #define UPPER 300 /* upper limit */
3. #define STEP 20       /* step size */
7
1. int main(void)
2. {
3.        int fahr;
11
1.        for (fahr = LOWER; fahr <= UPPER; fahr += STEP)
2.            printf("7,3d \t"/,6.1f\n", fahr, (5.0/9.0) * (fahr-32.0));
3. }
```

4-6 Symbolic constants are names that represent numerical constants. These are specified by #define, and mean that we can avoid littering our code with numbers. Numbers scattered through code are called "magic numbers" and should always be avoided. (There are rare exceptions where a literal constant is okay; the most common example is the number 0 to begin a loop over an array.)

1.　13 The for-loop has three components separated by two semicolons (;). The first initialises the loop, the second tests the condition (identical to the while-loop), and the third is an expression executed after each loop iteration. Notice that the actual conversion expression appears inside the printf() statement; an expression can be used wherever a variable can.

Style note. Variables should always begin with a lowercase letter, and multi-word names should be written either like_this or likeThis. Symbolic constants should always be UPPERCASE to distinguish them from variables.

## 1.　Organisation of the Text

This text is organised in a sequential fashion—from fundamentals to higher-level constructs and software design issues. The core language is covered in Chapters 2-5 and 7-13. (The material required to understand the examples in this chapter is covered in Chapters 2 and 3, and Sections 7.1, 7.2, and 8.2.)

Throughout the text, design techniques and good programming practice are emphasised to encourage a coding style conducive to building large-scale software systems. Good quality software not only works correctly, but is easy to read and understand, written in a clean, consistent style, and structured for future maintenance and extension. The basic process of program design is presented in Chapter 6.

Chapters 14 and 15 describe more advanced use of the C language, and are arguably the most interesting chapters of the book as they show how the individual language features combine to permit very powerful programming techniques. Chapter 14 discusses generic programming, which is the design of functions that can operate on a variety of different data types. Chapter 15 presents a selection of the fundamental data-structures that appear in many real programs and are both instructive and useful.

Chapter 16 provides a context for the book by describing how the ISO C language fits into the wider world of programming. Real world programming involves a great number of extensions beyond the standard language and C programmers must deal with other libraries, and possibly other languages, when writing real applications. Chapter 16 gives a taste of some of the issues.

# Chapter 2

## Types, Operators, and Expressions

*Variables and constants are the basic data objects manipulated in a program. Declarations list the variables to be used, and state what type they have and perhaps what their initial values are. Operators specify what is to be done to them. Expressions combine variables and constants to produce new values. The type of an object determines the set of values it can have and what operations can be performed on it [KR88, page 35].*

1. **Identifiers**

Identifiers (i.e., variable names, function names, etc) are made up of letters and digits, and are case-sensitive. The first character of an identifier must be a letter, which includes underscore ( ).* The C language has 32 keywords which are reserved and may not be used as identifiers (eg, int, while, etc). Furthermore, it is a good idea to avoid redefining identifiers used by the C standard library (such as standard function names, etc).

Style Note. Use lowercase for variable names and uppercase for symbolic constants. Local variable names should be short and external names should be longer and more descriptive. Variable names can begin with an underscore ( ), but this should be avoided as such names, by convention, are reserved for library implementations.

1. **Types**

C is a *typed* language. Each variable is given a specific type which defines what values it can represent, how its data is stored in memory, and what operations can be performed on it. By forcing the programmer to explicitly define a type for all variables and interfaces, the type system enables the compiler to catch type-mismatch errors, thereby preventing a significant source of bugs.

There are three basic types in the C language: characters, and integer and floating-point numbers. The numerical types come in several of sizes. Table 2.1 shows a list of C types and their typical

| C Data Types | |
| --- | --- |
| char | usually 8-bits (1 byte) |
| int | usually the natural word size for a machine or OS (e.g., 16, 32, 64 bits) |
| short int | at least 16-bits |
| long int | at least 32-bits |
| float | usually 32-bits |
| double | usually 64-bits |
| long double | usually at least 64-bits |

Table 2.1: C data types and their usual sizes.

sizes, although the sizes may vary from platform to platform. Nearly all current machines represent an int with at least 32-bits and many now use 64-bits. The size of an int generally represents the natural *word-size* of a machine; the native size with which the CPU handles instructions and data.

With regard to size, the standard merely states that a short int be at least 16-bits, a long int at least 32-bit, and

$$short\ int < int < long\ int$$

The standard says nothing about the size of floating-point numbers except that

$$float < double < long\ double.$$

A program to print the range of values for certain data types is shown below. The parameters such as INT_MIN can be found in standard headers limits.h and float.h (also see, for example, [KR88, page 257] or [HS95, pages 112, 118]).

```
#include <stdio.h>
#include <limits.h> /* integer specifications */
#include <float.h> /* floating-point specifications */

/* Look at range limits of certain types */
int main (void)
{
        printf("Integer range:\t%d\t%d\n", INT_MIN, INT_MAX);
        printf("Long range:\t%ld\t%ld\n", LONGMIN, LONGMAX);
        printf ("Float range: \t%e\t%e\n", FLT_MIN, FLT_MAX);
        printf ("Double range:\t%e\t%e\n", DBL_MIN, DBL_MAX);
        printf ("Long double range:\t%e\t%e\n", LDBL_MIN, LDBL_MAX);
        printf ("Float-Double epsilon:\t%e\t%e\n", FLT_EPSILON,
        DBL_EPSILON);

}
```

**Note.** The size of a type in number of characters (which is usually equivalent to number of bytes) can be found using the sizeof operator. This operator is not a function, although it often appears like one, but a keyword. It returns an unsigned integer of type size_t, which is defined in header-file stddef.h.

1.        sizeof(long), sizeof(float), sizeof(double));
2. }

The keywords short and long are known as *type qualifiers* because they affect the size of a basic int type. (The qualifier long may also be applied to type double.) Note, short and long, when used on their own as in

short a; long x;

are equivalent to writing short int and long int, respectively. Other type qualifiers are signed, unsigned, const, and volatile. The qualifiers signed or unsigned can apply to char or any integer type. A signed type may represent negative values; the most-significant-bit (MSB) of the number is its *sign-bit*, and the value is typically encoded in 2's-complement binary. An unsigned type is always non-negative, and the MSB is part of the numerical value—doubling the maximum representable value compared to an equivalent signed type. For example, a 16-bit signed short can represent the numbers -32768 to 32767 (i.e., $-2^{15}$ to $2^{15} - 1$), while a 16-bit unsigned short can represent the numbers 0 to 65535 (i.e., 0 to $2^{16} - 1$). (For more detail on the binary representation of signed and unsigned integers see Section 12.1.)

Note. Integer types are signed by default (e.g., writing short is equivalent to writing signed short int). However, whether plain char's are signed or unsigned by default is machine dependent.

The qualifier const means that the variable to which it refers cannot be changed.

const int DoesNotChange = 5;
DoesNotChange =6; /* Error: will not compile */

The qualifier volatile refers to variables whose value may change in a manner beyond the normal control of the program. This is useful for, say, multi-threaded programming or interfacing to hardware; topics which are beyond the scope of this text. The volatile qualifier is not directly relevant to standard-conforming C programs, and so will not be addressed further in this text.

Finally, there is a type called void, which specifies a "no value" type. It is used as an argument for functions that have no arguments, and as a return type for functions that return no value (see Chapter 4).

1.    **Constants**

Constants can have different types and representations. This section presents various constant types by example. First, an integer constant 1234 is of type int. An constant of type long int is suffixed by an L, 1234L; (integer constants too big for int are implicitly taken as long). An unsigned int is suffixed by a U, 1234U, and UL specifies unsigned long.

Integer constants may also be specified by octal (base 8) or hexadecimal (base 16) values, rather than decimal (base 10). Octal numbers are preceded by a 0 and hex by 0x. Thus, 1234 in decimal is equivalent to 02322 and 0x4D2. It is important to remember that these three constants represent exactly the same value (0101 1101 0010 in binary). For example, the following code

```
int x = 1234, y = 02322, z = 0x4D2;
printf("%d\t%o\t%x\n", x, x, x);
printf("%d\t%d\t%d\n", x, y, z);
```

prints

```
1234    2322    4d2
1234    1234    1234
```

Notice that C does not provide a direct binary representation. However, the hex form is very useful in practice as it breaks down binary into blocks of four bits (see Section 12.1).

Floating-point constants are specified by a decimal point after a number. For example, 1. and 1. are of type double, 3.14f and 2.f are of type float, and 7.L is of type long double. Floatingpoint numbers can also be written using scientific notation, such as 1.65e-2 (which is equivalent to 0.0165). Constant expressions, such as 3+7+9.2, are evaluated at compile-time and replaced by a single constant value, 19.2. Thus, constant expressions incur no runtime overhead.

Character constants, such as 'a', '\n', '7', are specified by single quotes. Character constants are noteworthy because they are, in fact, not of type char, but of int. Thus, sizeof('Z') will equal 4 on a 32-bit machine, not one. Most platforms represent characters using the ASCII character set, which associates the integers 0 to 127 with specific characters (e.g., the character 'T' is represented by the integer 84). Tables of the ASCII character set are readily found (see, for example, [HS95, page 421]).

There are certain characters that cannot be represented directly, but rather are denoted by an "escape sequence". It is important to recognise that these *escape characters* still represent single characters. A selection of key escape characters are the following: \0 for NUL (used to terminate character strings), \n for newline, \t for tab, \v for vertical tab, \\ for backslash, \' for single quotes, \" for double quotes, and \b for backspace.

String constants, such as "This is a string" are delimited by quotes (note, the quotes are not actually part of the string constant). They are implicitly appended with a terminating '\0' character. Thus, in memory, the above string constant would comprise the following character sequence: This is a string\0.

Note. It is important to differentiate between a character constant (e.g., 'X') and a NUL terminated string constant (e.g., "X"). The latter is the concatenation of two characters X\0. Note also that sizeof('X') is four (on a 32-bit machine) while sizeof("X") is two.

1.    **Symbolic Constants**

Symbolic constants represent constant values, from the set of constant types mentioned above, by a symbolic name. For example,

```
#define  BLOCK_SIZE   100
#define  TRACK_SIZE   (16*BLOCK_SIZE)
#define  HELLO        "Hello World\n"
#define  EXP          2.7183
```

Wherever a symbolic constant appears in the code, it is equivalent to direct text-replacement with the constant it defines. For example,

```
printf(HELLO);
```

prints the string Hello World. The reason for using symbolic constants rather than constant values directly, is that it prevents the proliferation of "magic numbers"—numerical constants scattered throughout the code. This is very important as magic numbers are error-prone and are the source of major difficulty when attempting to make code-changes. Symbolic constants keep constants together in one place so that making changes is easy and safe.

Note. The #define symbol, like the #include symbol for file inclusion, is a preprocessor command (see Section 10.2). As such, it is subject to different rules than the core C language. Importantly, the # must be the first character on a line; it must not be indented.

Another form of symbolic constant is an *enumeration,* which is a list of constant integer values. For example,

enum Boolean { FALSE, TRUE };

The *enumeration tag* Boolean defines the "type" of the enumeration list, such that a variable may be declared of the particular type.

enum Boolean x = FALSE;

If an enumeration list is defined without an explicit tag, it assumes the type int.[4] For example,

enum { RED=2, GREEN, BLUE, YELLOW=4, BLACK }; int y = BLUE;

The value of enumeration lists starts from zero by default, and increments by one for each subsequent member (e.g., FALSE is 0 and TRUE is 1). List members can also be given explicit integer values, and non-specified members are each one greater than the previous member (e.g., RED is 2, GREEN is 3, BLUE is 4, YELLOW is 4, and BLACK is 5).

Style Note. Symbolic constants and enumerations are by convention given uppercase names. This makes them distinct from variables and functions, which, according to good practice, should always begin with a lowercase letter. Variables qualified by const behave like constants[5] and so should also be identified with uppercase names, or with the first letter uppercase.

1.    **printf Conversion Specifiers**

The standard function printf() facilitates formatted text output. It merges numerical values of any type into a character string using various formatting operators and conversion specifiers.

printf("Character values %c %c %c\n", 'a', 'b', 'c'); printf("Some floating-point values %f %f %f\n", 3.556, 2e3, 40.1f); printf("Scientific notation %e %e %e\n", 3.556, 2e3, 40.1f); printf("%15.10s\n", "Hello World\n"); /* Right-justify string with space for

15 chars, print only first 10 letters */

A more complete discussion of printf() and its formatting fields and conversion specifiers is given in Section 13.1.1 (see also [KR88, pages 154, 243-246] and [HS95, page 372]).

Important. A conversion specifier and its associated variable must be of matching type. If they are not, the program will either print garbage or crash. For example,

printf("%f", 52); /* Mismatch: floating point specifier, integer value */

## 1.    **Declarations**

All variables must be *declared* before they are used. They must be declared at the top of a block (a section of code enclosed in brackets { and }) before any statements. They may be *initialised* by a constant or an expression when declared. The following are a set of example declarations.

a block */
3 uninitialised ints */ a char initialised with '\t' */ an uninitialised array of chars */ constant expression: 9 */ initialised with 9+5 = 14 */
    { /* bracket signifies top of int lower, upper, step; /* char tab = '\t';  /*
        char buf[10];        /*
        int m = 2+3+4;      /*
        int n = m + 5;       /*
        float limit = 9.34f; const double PI = 3.1416;

The general form of a declaration is

    <qualifier> <type> <identifier1> = <value1>, <identifier2> = <value2>, ... ;

where the assignment to an initial value is optional (see also Section 5.5).

## 1.    **Arithmetic Operations**

The arithmetic (or numerical) operators come in two varieties: unary and binary. The binary operators are plus +, minus —, multiply *, divide /, and the modulus operator %. The first four operators can be used on integer or floating-point types, although it is important to notice that integer division truncates any fractional part (e.g., 17/5 is equal to 3). The modulus operator is valid only for non-floating-point types (e.g., char, int, etc), and x % y produces the remainder from the division x / y (e.g., 18 % 7 is equal to 4).

Note. For negative integers, the direction of truncation for /, and the sign for the result of %, are implementation defined (i.e., they may have different results on different platforms). A portable work-around for this is shown in Section 10.3.2.

    The unary operators plus + and minus - can be used on integer or floating-point types, and are used as follows.

    int ispositive = +34;
    double isnegative = -56.3;

The unary + is a redundant operator as numbers are positive by default. It exists only for symmetry with the unary - operator.
    An important set of unary operators are the increment ++ and decrement -- operators. These operators add 1 to a variable and subtract 1 from a variable, respectively. Thus, the expression x++ is equivalent to x = x + 1. An unusual quality of ++ and — is that they may be used prefix ++x or postfix x++ with different characteristics. For example,

    double x = 3.2; double y = ++x; double z = x++;

In the first case, called preincrement, the value of x is increased to 4.2 and then assigned to y, which then also equals 4.2. In the second case, called postincrement, the value of x is first assigned to z, and subsequently increased by 1; so, z equals 4.2 and x equals 5.2.

The precedence of the arithmetic operators is as follows: ++, —, and unary + and — have the highest precedence; next comes *, /, and %; and finally, binary + and — have the lowest precedence.

```
int a=2, b=7, c=5, d=9;
printf("a*b + c*d = %d\n", a*b + c*d); /* prints a*b + c*d = 59 */
```

Two common errors can occur with numerical operations: divide-by-zero and overflow. The first occurs during a division operation z = x / y where y is equal to zero; this is the case for integer or floating-point division. Divide-by-zero errors can also occur with the modulus operator if the second operand is 0. The second error, overflow, occurs when the result of a mathematical operation cannot be represented by the result type. For example,

```
int z = x + 1;
```

will overflow if the value of x is the largest representable value of type int. The value of z following a divide-by-zero or overflow error will be erroneous, and may be different on different platforms.


1.     **Relational and Logical Operations**

There are six relational operators: greater-than >, less-than <, greater-than-or-equal-to >=, less- than-or-equal-to <=, equal-to == and not-equal-to !=. Relational expressions evaluate to 1 if they are TRUE and 0 if they are FALSE. For example, 2.1 < 7 evaluates to one, and x != x evaluates to zero.

Note. A very common programming error is to mistakenly type = (assignment) for == (equality). For example, consider a loop that is to execute while ever x == 3. If it is written as

```
while (x = 3) {
      /* various statements here */
}
```

then x will be assigned the value 3 and this value will be the loop conditional, which is always non-zero (and therefore TRUE) resulting in an infinite loop.

The three logical operators are AND && and OR || and NOT ! . All the relational and logical operators are binary except the ! , which is unary. The && and || operators connect pairs of conditional expressions, with && being TRUE only if both expressions are TRUE, and || being TRUE if either expression is TRUE. They can be used to chain together multiple expressions, as in the following example where, given the integer values a=1, b=2, c=3, d=3,

```
(a < b && b < c && c < d)    /* FALSE */
(a < b && b < c && c <= d) /* TRUE */
((a < b && b < c) || c < d) /* TRUE */
```

The order of evaluation of && and || is left-to-right, and evaluation stops as soon as the truth or falsehood of the result is known—leaving the remaining expressions unevaluated. This feature results in several common idioms in C programs. For example, given an array of length SIZE, it is incorrect to evaluate array[SIZE], which is one-beyond the end of the array. The idiom

```
i = 0;
while (i < SIZE && array[i] != val)
    ++i;
```

ensures that, when i == SIZE, the conditional expression terminates before evaluating array[i].

The unary operator ! simply converts a non-zero expression to zero and vice-versa. For example, the statement

```
if (!valid) x = y;
```

performs the assignment x = y only if valid equals 0. The unary ! tends to be used infrequently as it can lead to obscure code, and typically == or != provide a more readable alternative.

```
if (valid == 0)
    x = y;
```

The precedence of the relational and logical operators is lower than the arithmetic operators, except for the unary ! , which has equal precedence to the unary + and -. Of the others, >, <, >=, and <= have highest precedence; followed by == and !=; then &&; and finally, ||.

Style Note. C has precedence rules for all its operators (e.g., see the precedence tables in [KR88, page 53]). However, for correctness and readability, it is good practice to make minimal use of these rules (e.g., * and / are evaluated before + and -) and use parentheses everywhere else.

The following example is a segment of code where the intuitive precedence is not correct, and the code is faulty. This code is intended to copy the characters of a string t to a character array s, an operation which is complete when the terminating '\0' is copied.

```
while (s[i] = t[i] != '\0')
    ++i;
```

However, the != has higher precedence than the =, and so s[i] will not be assigned t[i] but the result of t[i] != '\0', which is 1 except for the final iteration when it will be 0. The correct result is obtained using parentheses.

```
while ((s[i] = t[i]) != '\0')
    ++i;
```

## 1.   **Bitwise Operators**

C possesses a number if bitwise operators that permit operations on individual bits (i.e., binary 1s and 0s). These are essential for low-level programming, such as controlling hardware. We discuss bitwise operators in detail in Chapter 12, but mention them here to prevent confusion with the logical operators, which bear a superficial resemblance.

The operators are the bitwise AND &, bitwise OR |, bitwise exclusive OR ", left shift <<, right shift >>, and one's complement operator ~. It is important to realise that & is not &&, | is not ||, and >> does not mean "much-greater-than". The purpose and usage of the logical and bitwise operators are quite disparate and may not be used interchangeably.

# 1. Assignment Operators

Expressions involving the arithmetic or bitwise operators often involve the assignment operator = (for example, z = x + y). Sometimes in these expressions, the left-hand-side variable is repeated immediately on the right (e.g., x = x + y). These types of expression can be written in the compressed form x += y, where the operator += is called an *assignment operator.*

   The binary arithmetic operators, +, —, *, /, and % each have a corresponding assignment operator +=, -=, *=, /=, and %=. Thus, we can write x *= y + 1 rather than x = x * (y + 1). For completeness, we mention also the bitwise assignment operators: &=, |=, "=, <<=, and >>=. We return to the bitwise operators in Chapter 12.

# 1. Type Conversions and Casts

*When an operator has operands of different types, they are converted to a common type according to a small number of rules [KR88, page 42].*

   For a binary expression such as a * b, the following rules are followed (assuming neither operand is unsigned):

- If either operand is long double, convert the other to long double.
- Otherwise, if either operand is double, convert the other to double.
- Otherwise, if either operand is float, convert the other to float.
- Otherwise, convert char and short to int, and, if either operand is long, convert the other to long.

If the two operands consist of a signed and an unsigned version of the same type, then the signed operand will be promoted to unsigned, with strange results if the previously signed value was negative.

   A simple example of type promotion is shown in the following code.

```
short a = 5; int b = 10; float c =
23.1f; double d = c + a*b;
```

Here the multiply is performed first, so a is promoted to int and multiplied with b. The integer result of this expression is promoted to float and added to c. This result is then promoted to double and assigned to d.

Note. The promotion from char to int is implementation-dependent, since whether a plain char is signed or unsigned depends on the compiler. Some platforms will perform "sign extension" if the left-most bit is 1, while others will fill the high-order bits with zeros—so the value is always positive.

   Assignment to a "narrower" operand is possible, although information may be lost. Conversion to a narrower type should elicit a warning from good compilers. Conversion from a larger integer to a smaller one results in truncation of the higher-order bits, and conversion from floating-point to integer causes truncation of any fractional part. For example,

```
int iresult = 0.5 + 3/5.0;
```

The division 3/5.0 is promoted to type double so that the final summation equals 1.1. The result then is truncated to 1 in the assignment to iresult. Note, a conversion from double to float is implementation dependent and might be either truncated or rounded.

   Narrowing conversions should be avoided. For the cases where they are necessary, they should be made explicit by a *cast*. For example, int iresult = (int)(0.5 + 3/5.0);

Casts can also be used to coerce a conversion, such as going against the promotion rules specified above. For example, the expression

result = (float)5.0 + 3.f;

will add the two terms as float's rather than double's.

## Chapter 3

## Branching and Iteration

The C language provides three types of decision-making constructs: if-else, the *conditional expression* ?:, and the switch statement. It also provides three looping constructs: while, do-while, and for. And it has the infamous goto, which is capable of both non-conditional branching and looping.

1. **If-Else**

The basic if statement tests a conditional expression and, if it is non-zero (i.e., TRUE), executes the subsequent statement. For example, in this code segment

if (a < b) b = a;

the assignment b = a will only occur if a is less-than b. The else statement deals with the alternative case where the conditional expression is 0 (i.e., FALSE).

```
if (a < b) b = a;
else
      b += 7;
```

The if-else statement can also command multiple statements by wrapping them in braces. Statements so grouped are called a *compound statement,* or *block,* and they are syntactically equivalent to a single statement.

```
if (a < b) { b = a; a
      *= 2;
}
else {
      b += 7;
      --a;
}
```

It is possible to chain if-else statements if the following form

```
if (expression)
      statement;
else if (expression)
      statement;
else if (expression)
      statement;
else
```

statement;

This chain is evaluated from the top and, if a particular if-conditional is TRUE, then its statement is executed and the chain is terminated. On the other hand, if the conditional is FALSE, the next if-conditional is tested. If all the conditionals evaluate to FALSE, then the final else statement is executed as a default. (Note, the final else is optional and, if it is missing, the default action is no action.)

An example if-else chain is shown below. This code segment performs integer division on the first k elements of an array of integers num[SIZE]. The first two if-statements do error-checking, and the final else does the actual calculation. Notice that the else is a compound statement, and that a variable (int i) is declared there; variables may be declared at the top of any block, and their *scope* is local to that block.

```
if (k < 0 || k > SIZE)
        printf("Error: Invalid number of elements (out-of-bounds).\n"); else
if (denom == 0)
        printf("Error: Denominator is zero.\n"); else {
        int i;
        printf("Result of division by %d: ", denom); for (i = 0; i < k; ++i)
            printf("%d ", num[i]/denom);
        printf("\n");
}
```

Note. A common mistake with if-else blocks is the "dangling else problem". For example, consider the following nested-if statement.

```
if (a < b)
        if (m != 0) b = a;
else
        a = m;
```

The intention of the programmer, as indicated by the indentation, is that the else corresponds to the outer if statement. However, it actually belongs to the inner if statement. Desired association can be enforced by brackets.

```
if (a < b) {
        if (m != 0) b = a;
}
else
        a = m;
```

1.      **?: Conditional Expression**

The conditional expression is a ternary operator; that is, it takes three operands. It has the following form

(expression 1) ? (expression 2) : (expression 3)

If the first expression is TRUE (i.e., non-zero), the second expression is evaluated, otherwise the third is evaluated. Thus, the result of the ternary expression will be the result of either the second or third expressions, respectively. For example, to calculate the maximum of two values,

c = (a > b) ? a : b; /* c = max(a,b) */

As a branching construct, the ?: operator appears far less frequently than the if-else and switch constructs.

# 1. Switch

*The switch statement is a multi-way decision that tests whether an expression matches one of a number of constant integer values, and branches accordingly [KR88, page 58].*

The general form of the switch statement is as follows.

```
switch (expression) {
    case   const-int-expr:   statements
    case   const-int-expr:   statements
    default: statements
}
```

On evaluating the expression, if it matches one of the set of constant integer expressions, the switch branches to the matching case label and executes the statements following that point. Otherwise it jumps to the default label and executes its statements. The default label is optional, and if it does not exist, and none of the case labels match, the switch simply performs no action.

Note. The default label is typically the last label in the block. While this is good practice in general, it is not mandatory, and case labels may appear below default.

The statements following a case label are executed until terminated by a break statement, which causes an immediate exit from the switch block. However, if a break is not encountered, execution will flow on through to the next cases until the end of the block. This is termed *fall through* and is the default behaviour in a switch. Fall through is rarely used because it is difficult to code correctly; it should be used with caution.

Style Note. It is generally good practice to have a default label even when it is not necessary, even if it just contains an assert to catch logical errors (i.e., program bugs). Also, fall-through is much less common than break, and every case label should either end with a break or have a /* Fall Through */ comment to make ones intentions explicit. Finally, it is wise to put a break after the last case in the block, even though it is not logically necessary. Some day additional cases might be added to the end and this practice will prevent unexpected bugs.

It is worth mentioning here that all the control structures—if-else, ?:, while, do-while, and for—can be *nested*, which means that they can exist within other control statements. The switch- statement is no exception, and the statements following a case label may include a switch or other control structure. For example, the following code-structure is legitimate.

```
if (expression)
    while (expression)
        switch(integer expression) {
        case A1:
            switch(integer expression) {
                case B1:   statements
                case B2:   statements
                case B3:   statements
```

```
        }
    case A2: statements
    default:  statements
    }
```

The following example converts the value of a double variable angle to normalised radians (i.e., —n < angle < n). The original angle representation is either degrees or radians, as indicated by the integer angletype, and DEG, RAD, and PI are symbolic constants.

```
                    switch (angletype)
{
case DEG:
    angle *= PI / 180.0; /* convert to radians */
    /* fall through */

case RAD:
    while (angle > PI) /* normalise radians */ angle
    -= 2.0*PI; while (angle < -PI) angle += 2.0*PI;
    break;

default:
    printf("Error: Invalid type\n"); break;
}
```

## 1.    **While Loops**

The while loop has the general form

```
            while (expression)
            statement;
```

If the conditional expression is TRUE, then the while will execute the following statement, after which it will reevaluate the conditional. It continues this iteration while ever the conditional remains TRUE. As with the if-else statement, the while loop can execute multiple statements as a block by enclosing them in braces.

For example, the following code segment computes the *greatest common divisor* (GCD) of two positive integers m and n (i.e., the maximum value that will divide both m and n). The loop iterates until the value of n becomes 0, at which point the GCD is the value of m.

```
while (n) {
    int tmp = n;
    n = m%n;
    m = tmp;
}
```

## 1.    **Do-While Loops**

The do-while loop has the general

form do

```
            statement;
```

while (expression);

Its behaviour is virtually the same as the while loop except that it always executes the statement at least once. The statement is executed first and then the conditional expression is evaluated to decide upon further iteration. Thus, the body of a while loop is executed zero or more times, and the body of a do-while loop is executed one or more times.

Style note. It is good form to always put braces around the do-while body, even when it consists of only one statement. This prevents the while part from being mistaken for the beginning of a while loop.

The following code example takes a non-negative integer val and prints it in reverse order. The use of a do-while means that 0 can be printed without needing extra special-case code.

```
do
{
    printf("%d", val % 10);
    val /= 10;
} while (val != 0);
```

## 1.    **For Loops**

The for loop has the general form

```
for (expr1; expr2; expr3)
    statement;
```

Its behaviour is equivalent to a while loop with the following arrangement of expressions.

```
expr1;
while (expr2) { statement;
    expr3;
}
```

In the for loop, expressions 1, 2, and 3 are optional, although the semicolons must remain. If expressions 1 or 3 are not there, then the loop simple behaves like the while loop above without expressions 1 or 3. If expression 2 is omitted, then the conditional is always TRUE, and an infinite loop results.

```
for (;;) /* infinite loop */
    statement;
```

Note. It is possible to stack several expressions in the various parts of the for loop using the *comma operator*. The comma operator enables multiple statements to appear as a single statement without having to enclose them with braces. However, it should be used sparingly, and is most suited for situations like the following example. This example reverses a character string in-place. The first loop finds the end of the string, and the second loop performs the reversing operation by swapping characters.

```
for (j=0; str[j] != '\0'; ++j)

for (i=0, --j; i < j; ++i, --j) { tmp =
    str[i]; str[i] = str[j]; str[j] =
    tmp;
}
```

## 1. **Break and Continue**

As seen previously, break can be used to branch out of a switch-statement. It may also be used to branch out of any of the iterative constructs. Thus, a break may be used to terminate the execution of a switch, while, do-while, or for. It is important to realise that a break will only branch out of an inner-most enclosing block, and transfers program-flow to the first statement following the block. For example, consider a nested while-loop.

```
while (expression) {
    while (expression) { if
(expression) break; statements
    }
    statements
}
```

Here the break will terminate the inner while-loop and proceed to execute the statements of the outer while-loop.

This next example (adapted from [HS95, page 253]) shows a fast technique for finding the smallest element in an array of length SIZE. A break is used to terminate the infinite outer while-loop.

```
i = SIZE;
temp = smallest = array[0]; while
(1) {
    while (array[—i] > smallest)
    
    if (i == 0) break;
    array[0] = smallest = array[i];
}
array[0] = temp;
```

The continue-statement operates on loops only; it does not operate on switch. For while and do-while it causes transfer of program-control immediately to the conditional test, which is reevaluated for the next iteration. The same action occurs for a for-loop after first executing the increment expression (i.e., expression 3). Note that, as with break, continue acts on the inner-most enclosing block of a nested loop.

> *The* continue *statement is often used when the part of the loop that follows is complicated, so that reversing a test and indenting another level would nest the program too deeply [KR88, page 65].*

The following example shows the outline of a code-segment that performs operations on the positive elements of an array but skips the negative elements. The continue provides a concise means for ignoring the negative values.

```
for (i = 0; i<SIZE ; ++i) {
    if (array[i] < 0) /* skip -ve elements */
        continue;

    /* process +ve elements */
}
```

Note. Both break and continue have no effect on an if-statement. A common misconception is that break can be used to jump out of an if compound statement. For example, given a nested construct of the form,

```
while (expression) {
statements if (expression)
{ statements if
(expression) break;
statements
}
    statements after if
}
statements after loop
```

it is commonly presumed that the break will transfer control to the statements after if, whereas it will actually transfer control to the statements after loop.

## 1.    **Goto**

The goto statement has a well-deserved reputation for being able to produce unreadable "spaghetti" code. It is almost never necessary to use one, and they should be avoided in general. However, on rare occasions they are convenient and safe. A goto statement provides the ability to jump to a *named-label* anywhere within the same function.
    One situation where a goto can be useful is if it becomes necessary to break out of a deeply nested structure, such as nested loops. A break statement cannot do this as it can only break out of one level at a time. The following example gives the basic idea.

```
1.  int main(void)
2.  /* Demonstrate a legitimate use of goto (adapted from K&R page 66). This
    example is contrived, but the idea is to
3.  * find a common element in two arrays. In the process, we demonstrate a couple
    of useful standard library functions. */
4.  {
5.      char a[SIZE], b[SIZE];
6.      int i, j;
```

```
14
1.      /* Initialise arrays so they are different from each other */
2.      memset(a, VAL1, SIZE);
3.      memset(b, VAL2, SIZE);
```

```
18
1.      /* Set a random element in each array to VALUE */
2.      a[rand()%SIZE] = VAL3;
3.      b[rand()%SIZE] = VAL3;
```

```
22
1.      /* Search for location of common elements */
2.      for (i=0; i<SIZE; ++i)
3.          for (j=0; j<SIZE; ++j)
4.              if (a[i] == b[j])
5.                  goto found;
```

```
28
1.      /* Error: match not found */
2.      printf("Did not find any common elements! !\n");
3.      return 0;
```

```
32
1.  found: /* Results on success */
```

2.    printf("a[%,d]= %,c      and        b['/,d]    =      %,c\n", i, a[i], j,
        b[j]);
3.  }

# Chapter 4

# Functions

> *Functions break large computing tasks into smaller ones, and enable people to build on what others have done instead of starting over from scratch. Appropriate functions hide details of operation from parts of the program that don't need to know them, thus clarifying the whole, and easing the pain of making changes [KR88, page 67].*

Functions are fundamental to writing modular code. They provide the basic mechanism for enclosing low-level source code, hiding algorithmic details and presenting instead an interface that describes more intuitively what the code actually does. Functions present a higher level of abstraction and facilitate a divide-and-conquer strategy for program decomposition. When combined with file-modular design (see Sections 5.7 and 11.6), functions make it possible to build and maintain large-scale software systems without being overwhelmed by complexity.

## 1.    Function Prototypes

A function must be declared before it is used. This means that either the function declaration or definition must exist in the source file above the place where it is first called by some other function.

A function declaration, or prototype, is an interface specification. It states the function name, the number and type of input arguments, and the return value type. It enables the compiler to perform type-checking—to ensure the argument types being passed to the function match the interface definition—which catches many coding errors at compile time. Some example prototypes are as follows.

```
void some_procedure(void); int
string_length(char *str);
double point_distance(double, double, double, double);
```

Notice that the variable names are optional in the declaration, only the types matter. However, variable names can help clarify how a function should be used.

# 1. **Function Definition**

A function definition contains the actual workings of the function—the declarations and statements of the function algorithm. The function is passed a number of input parameters (or arguments) and may return a value, as specified by its interface definition.

Function arguments are passed by a transaction termed "pass-by-value". This means that the function receives a local *copy* of each input variable, not the variable itself. Thus, any changes made to the local variable will not affect the value of the variable in the calling function. For example,

```
int myfunc(int x, int y)
/* This function takes two int arguments, and returns an int. */
{
    x *= 3;
    ++y;
    return x + y;
}

void caller_func(void)
/* A function that calls myfunc() */
{
    int a=1, b=2, c, d;

    c = myfunc(a,b); /* c = 6 */ d = a + b;      /*d = 3*/
}
```

In this case, the values passed to myfunc() are x=1 and y=2, respectively, and these are changed to x=3 and y=3 in the subsequent statements. However, the values of a and b are unaffected and d = 1+2 = 3.

To obtain a value from a function, it may specify a return value. The calling function is free to ignore the return value, but it is good practice to make this explicit by putting a (void) cast in front of the call. For example,

```
int an_algorithm(int, int); /* Prototype: two int arguments, and returns an int. */

void caller_func(void)
{
    int a=1, b=2, c;
    c = an_algorithm(a,b); /* use return value */
    an_algorithm(a,b);          /* ignore   return value
    (implicitly) */
    (void)an_algorithm(a,b); /* ignore return value (explicitly) */
}

int an_algorithm(int x, int y)
{
    return x*2 + x/y;
}
```

The return value can be of any type, but there is a limitation that any function may only have at most one return value. To return multiple values it is necessary to either (i) return a compound type in the form of struct, or (ii) directly manipulate the values of the input variables using an approach termed "pass-by-reference". These methods are discussed in Sections 11.2 and 7.3, respectively.

While a function can only have one return *value,* it may possess several return statements. These define multiple exit points from the function, from which program-control returns to the next statement of the calling function. If a function is to return a value of a certain type, all return statements must return a value of that type. But, if a function does not return a value, then an empty return; suffices, and this may be omitted altogether for a no-value return occurring at the end of the function block.

```
1 int isleapyear (int year)
   /* Return true if year is a leap-year */
   {
           if( year % 4 ) return 0; /* not divisible
           by 4 */ if( year % 100 ) return 1; /*
           divisible by 4, but not 100 */ if( year
           % 400 ) return 0; /* divisible by 100,
           but not 400 */ return 1; /* divisible
           by 400 */
   }
```

Functions in C are recursive, which means that they can call themselves. Recursion tends to be less efficient than iterative code (i.e., code that uses loop-constructs), but in some cases may facilitate more elegant, easier to read code. The following code examples show two simple functions with both iterative and recursive implementations. The first calculates the greatest common divisor of two positive integers m and n, and the second computes the factorial of a non-negative integer n.

```
/* Iterative GCD: Returns the greatest common divisor of m and n. */
int gcd (int m, int n)
{
    while (n) {
        int tmp = n;
        n = m % n;
        m
```

```
                =
                t
                m
                p
                i
        }
        return m;
}

/* Recursive GCD */
int gcdr (int m, int n)
{
        if (n==0) return m; return gcdr(n,
        m%n);
}
```

Notice that the factorial functions below incorporate argument checking via the standard library macro assert, which causes the program to terminate with an error message if the conditional expression is FALSE.

## 1.    Benefits of Functions

Novice programmers tend to pack all their code into main(), which soon becomes unmanageable. Scalable software design involves breaking a problem into sub-problems, which can each be tackled separately. Functions are the key to enabling such a division and separation of concerns.

Writing programs as a collection of functions has manifold benefits, including the following.

- Functions allow a program to be split into a set of subproblems which, in turn, may be further split into smaller subproblems. This divide-and-conquer approach means that small parts of the program can be written, tested, and debugged in isolation without interfering with other parts of the program.

- Functions can wrap-up difficult algorithms in a simple and intuitive interface, hiding the implementation details, and enabling a higher-level view of the algorithm's purpose and use.

- Functions avoid code duplication. If a particular segment of code is required in several places, a function provides a tidy means for writing the code only once. This is of considerable benefit if the code segment is later altered.

Consider the following examples. The function names and interfaces give a much higher-level idea of the code's purpose than does the code itself, and the code is readily reusable.

```
int toupper (int c)
/* Convert lowercase letters to uppercase, leaving all other characters unchanged.
Works correctly
 • only for character sets with consecutive letters, such as ASCII. */
{
        if (c >= 'a'
        && c <= 'z')
        c += 'A' —
```

```
        'a'; return c;
}

int isdigit(int c)
/* Return 1 if c represents an integer character ('0' to '9'). This function only
works if the character
•   codes for 0 to 9 are consecutive, which is the case for ASCII and EBCDIC
 character sets. */
{
        return c >= '0' && c <= '9';
}

void strcpy (char *s, char *t)
/* Copy character-by-character the string t to the character array s. Copying
ceases once the terminating
•   '\0' has been copied. */
{
        int i=0;
        while ((s[i] = t[i]) != '\0')
                ++i;
}

double asinh(double x)
/* Compute the inverse hyperbolic sine of an angle x, where x is in radians and -PI
<= x <= PI. */
{
        return log(x + sqrt(x * x + 1.0));
}
```

As a more complex example, consider the function getline() below. This function reads a line of characters from standard-input (usually the keyboard) and stores it in a character buffer. Notice that this function, in turn, calls the standard library function getchar(), which gets a single character from standard input. The relative simplicity of the function interface of getline() compared to its definition is immediately apparent.

```
/* Get a line of data from stdin and store in a character array, s, of size,
 len. Return the length of the line. * Algorithm from K&R page 69. */
int getline(char s[], int len)
{
        int i=0, c;

        /* Loop until: (i) buffer full, (ii) no more input available, or (iii)
         the end-of-line is reached (marked * by newline character). */
        while ( -len > 0 && (c=getchar()) != EOF && c != '\n')
                s[i++] = c;
        if (c == '\n') /* loop terminated by end-of-line, want to
                keep newline character */ s[i++] = c;
        s[i] = '\0'; /* mark end-of-string */
        return i;
}
```

1.      **Designing For Errors**

When writing programs, and especially when designing functions, it is important to perform appropriate error-checking. This section discusses two possible actions for terminal errors, assert() and exit(), and also the use of function return values as a mechanism for reporting non-terminal errors to calling functions.

The standard library macro assert() is used to catch logical errors (i.e., coding bugs, errors that cannot happen in a bug-free program). Situations that "can't happen" regularly do happen, and assert() is an excellent means for weeding out these often subtle bugs. The form of assert() is as follows,

    assert(expression);

where the expression is a conditional test with non-zero being TRUE and zero being FALSE. If the expression is FALSE, then an error has occurred and assert() prints an error message and terminates the program. For example, the expression

    assert(idx>=0 && idx<size);

will terminate the program if idx is outside the specified bounds. A common use of assert() is within function definitions to ensure that the calling program uses it correctly. For example, int isprime(int val)
/* Brute-force algorithm to check for primeness */ {
int i;

5
assert(val >= 2);
6

```
1.      for (i = 2; i < val; ++i)
2.          if (val % i == o)
3.              return 0;
4.      return 1;
5. }
```

Another common practice is to place an assert() in the final else of an if-else chain or the default case of a switch when the default condition is not supposed to ever occur.

```
switch (expression)
{
case        label1:
statements;   break;
case        label2:
statements;   break;
default: assert(0); /*
can't happen */
}
```

Being a macro, assert() is processed by the C preprocessor, which performs text-replacement on the source code before it is parsed by the compiler. If the build is in debug-mode, the preprocessor transforms the assert() into a conditional that, if FALSE, prints a message of the form

    Assertion failed: <expression>, file <file name>, line <line number>

and terminates the program. But, if the build is in release-mode (i.e., the non-debug version of the program), then the preprocessor transforms the assert() into nothing—the assertion is ignored. Thus, assertion statements have no effect on the efficiency on release code.

Note. Assertions greatly assist the code debugging process and incur no runtime penalty on release- version code. Use them liberally.

The standard library function exit() is used to terminate a program either as a normal completion (e.g., in response to a user typing "quit"),

```
if (user_input == 'q') exit(0);
```

or upon encountering a non-recoverable error (e.g., insufficient memory to complete a dynamic memory request).

```
int* mem = (int*) malloc(50 * sizeof(int)); if (mem ==
NULL) exit(1);
```

The form of exit() is

```
void exit(int status);
```

where status is the exit-status of the program, which is returned to the calling environment. The value 0 indicates a successful termination and a non-zero value indicates an abnormal termination. (Also, the standard defines two symbolic constants EXIT_SUCCESS and EXIT_FAILURE for this purpose.)
The need to terminate a program in response to a non-recoverable error is not a bug; it can occur in a bug-free program. For example, requesting dynamic memory or opening a file,

```
FILE* pfile =
fopenO'myfile.txt", "r"); if
(pfile == NULL) exit(1);
```

is dependent on the availability of resources outside of the program control. As such, exit() statements will remain in release-version code. Use exit() sparingly—only when the error is terminal, and never inside a function that is designed to be reusable (i.e., functions not tailored to a specific program). Functions designed for reuse should return an error flag to allow the calling function to determine an appropriate action.
Recognising the difference between situations that require assert() (logical errors caused by coding bugs), and those that require exit() (runtime errors outside the control of the program), is primarily a matter of programming experience.

Note. The function exit() performs various cleanup operations before killing the program (e.g., flushing output streams and calling functions registered with atexit()). A stronger form of termination function is abort(), which kills the program without any cleanup; abort() should be avoided in general.

Function return values are often used to report errors to the calling function. The return value might either be used exclusively as a status value,

```
int function_returns_status (arguments)
{
    statements
    if (success) return 0; return 1;
}
```

or might return a certain range of values in normal circumstances, and a special value in the case of an error. For example,

```
int function_returns_value (arguments)
{
    int val; statements
    if (error) return -1;
    return val; /* normal values are non-negative */
}
```

The idea of a return value is to inform the calling function that an error has occurred, and the calling function is responsible for deciding what action is appropriate. For example, an appropriate action might be to ignore bad input, or to print a message and continue, or, in the worst case, to terminate the program.

In particular, many of the standard library functions return error values. It is common practice in toy programs to ignore function return values, but production code should always check and respond suitably. In addition, the standard library defines a global error variable errno, which is used by some standard functions to specify what kind of error has occurred. Standard functions that use errno will typically return a value indicating an error has occurred, and the calling function should check errno to determine the type of error.

## 1.    Interface Design

Good design of function interfaces is a somewhat nebulous topic, but there are some fundamental principles that are generally applicable.

- Functions should be self-contained and accessible only via well-defined interfaces. It is usually bad practice to expose function internals. That is, an interface should expose an algorithm's purpose, not an algorithm's implementation. Functions are an abstraction mechanism that allow code to be understood at a higher level.

- Function dependences should be avoided or minimised. That is, it is desirable to minimise the effect that changing one function will have upon another. Ideally, a function can be altered, enhanced, debugged, etc, independently, with no effect on the operation of other functions.

- A function should perform a single specific task. Avoid writing functions that perform several tasks; it is better to split such a function into several functions, and later combine them in a "wrapper" function, if required. Wrapper functions are useful for ensuring that a set of related functions are called in a specific sequence.

- Function interfaces should be minimal. It should have only the arguments necessary for its specific task, and should avoid extraneous "bells and whistles" features.

- A good interface should be intuitive to use.

## 1.    The Standard Library

The standard library has a large number of functions (about 145) which provide many commonly- used routines and operations. These functions exist on all standard-conforming systems; they are portable and correct, so use them before writing implementations of your own. Also, the standard library functions are a good example of quality interface design. Note the use of short, descriptive function names, and intuitive, minimal interfaces.

It pays to become familiar with the standard library. Learn what functions are available and their various purposes. The following is a selection of particularly useful functions listed by category.

- Mathematical functions. sqrt, pow, sin, cos, tan.

- Manipulating characters. isdigit, isalpha, isspace, toupper, tolower.

- Manipulating strings. strlen, strcpy, strcmp, strcat, strstr, strtok.

- Formatted input and output. printf, scanf, sprintf, sscanf.

- File input and output. fopen, fclose, fgets, getchar, fseek.

- Error handling. assert, exit.

- Time and date functions. clock, time, difftime.

- Sort and search. qsort, bsearch.

- Low-level memory operations. memcpy, memset.

## Chapter 5

## Scope and Extent

The *scope* of a name refers to the part of the program within which the name can be used. That is, it describes the *visibility* of an identifier within the program. The *extent* of a variable or function refers to its *lifetime* in terms of when memory is allocated to store it, and when that memory is released.

The rules of scope and extent affect the way functions and data interact, and are central to the design of C programs. This chapter examines the various *storage classes* that control these properties. The focus is on the way in which control of scope and extent facilitate the writing of modular programs, and particularly the implementation of multiple-file programs.

1.    **Local Scope and Automatic Extent**

A variable declared within a function has *local scope* by default. This means that it is local to the block in which it is defined, where a block is a code segment enclosed in braces {...}. Function arguments also have local scope. For example, in the following function

```
void afunction(int a, int b)
{
    d
    o
    u
```

```
ble val;
statements
{
    int val2 = 5;
    statements
} /* val2 goes out-of-scope here */
statements
} /* a, b, val go out-of-scope here */
```

the variables a, b, val, and val2 all have local scope. The visibility of a local variable is the block in which it is defined. Thus local variables with the same name defined in different blocks or functions are unrelated.

A local variable has *automatic extent,* which means that its lifetime is from the point it is defined until the end of its block. At the point it is defined, memory is allocated for it on the "stack"; this memory is managed automatically by the compiler. If the variable is not explicitly initialised, then it will hold an undefined value (e.g., in the above, val has an arbitrary value, while val2 is initialised to 5). It is often good practice to initialise a local variable when it is declared. At the end of the block, the variable is destroyed and the memory recovered; the variable is said to go "out-of-scope".

## 1. External Scope and Static Extent

*External variables are defined outside of any function, and are thus potentially available to many functions. Functions themselves are always external, because C does not allow functions to be defined inside other functions [KR88, page 73].*

A variable defined outside of any function is an *external* variable, by default. External variables and functions are visible over the entire (possibly multi-file) program; they have *external scope* (also called *program scope*). This means that a function may be called from any function in the program, and an external variable may be accessed or changed by any function. However, it is necessary to first declare a variable or function in each file before it is used.

The extern keyword is used to *declare* the existence of an external variable in one file when it is *defined* in another. Function prototypes may also be preceded by extern, but this is not essential as they are external by default. It is important to note the distinction between *declaration* and *definition*. A declaration refers to the specification of a variable or function, in particular its name and type. A definition is also a specification, but additionally involves the allocation of storage. A variable or function may be declared multiple times in a program (provided the declarations are non-conflicting) but may be defined only once. An example of external variables and functions shared across two source-files is shown below.

```
        File one.c:
external variable definition */
external variable declaration (defined elsewhere) */ external function prototype (declaration) */
        int globalvar;              /*
        extern double myvariable; /* void myfunc(int idx);      /*

        File two.c:
        double myvariable = 3.2; /* external variable definition */

        void myfunc(int idx)
        /* Function definition */
        {
            extern int globalvar; /* external variable declaration */

        }
```

Note. Each source file (i.e., a file with filename suffixed by .c) is compiled to form an object module. These are later combined by the linker to form a complete executable program. The identifiers of external variables and functions are visible to the linker, allowing them to be shared across separate object modules, and are said to have "external linkage". The identifiers of non-external variables and functions are not visible to the linker, and so are private to a single source-file.

External variables and functions have *static extent*. This means that they are allocated memory and exist before the program starts—before the execution of main()—and continue to exist until the program terminates. External variables that are not initialised explicitly are given the default value of zero; (this is different to local variables, which have arbitrary initial values by default). The value of an external variable is retained from one function call to the next.

External variables are sometimes used as a convenient mechanism for avoiding long argument lists. They provide an alternative to function arguments and return values for communicating data between functions. They may also permit more natural semantics if two functions operate on the same data, but neither calls the other.

The following example (from [KR88, page 79]) shows a situation where global variables might be convenient. Suppose you wish to get input from the keyboard one character at a time; the standard function getchar() provides this service. However, suppose you read in some characters and decide you are not yet ready to process them, and wish to push them back onto the input stream for a later time. This cannot be done directly, but can be simulated by storing the pushed-back characters in a buffer, and writing two functions that get and unget the characters, respectively.

```
#define BUFSIZE 100

char buffer[BUFSIZE]; /* buffer for pushed-back
characters */ int bufidx =0; /* buffer index */

int getch(void)
/* Get a character from stdin. */
{
    if (bufidx > 0) /* get pushed-back data
first */ return buffer[—bufidx]; return
getchar();
}

int ungetch(int c)
/* Simulate pushing a character back onto input stream */
{
    if (bufidx >= BUFSIZE) return -1; /* error: buffer
full */ buffer[bufidx++] = c; return 0;
}
```

The problem with external variables is that they tend to expose function internals, which can lead to strong dependencies between functions. Two functions are said to be "tightly coupled" if changes made to one function forces changes on the other. This style of code violates the modular design principle of decoupled functions accessible only via well-defined interfaces. A further problem with external variables is that, since their scope is over the entire multi-file program, it is easy to write code where the same identifier is used to define two different external variables. Overuse of external variables is said to "clutter the global name-space", and naming conflicts can arise affecting both functions and variables, as shown in the following example.

File one.c:
extern double myvariable;
float myname;
void myfunc(int idx);

File two.c:
extern int myvariable; char myname(int c); int myfunc(int idx);

As a rule, external variables are easy to overuse and should be avoided where possible.


1.      **The static Storage Class Specifier**

The keyword static is a storage class specifier, but it is perhaps better viewed as a storage class *qualifier* as it imparts different properties depending on whether an object is a local variable, an
external variable, or a function. Local variables keep their local visibility but gain static extent. They are initialised to zero by default and retain their values between function calls.

int increment(void)
{
        static int local_static; /* local scope, static extent, initial value 0 */ return local_static++; /* 1st call will return: 0, 2nd: 1, 3rd: 2, ... */
}

External variables and functions that are qualified as static obtain *file scope*, which means their visibility is limited to a single source file. Their names are not exported to the linker and are not visible to object modules of other source files. This prevents unwanted access by code in other parts of the program and reduces the risk of naming conflicts. For example, the following declarations are unrelated and non-conflicting.

File one.c:
static double
myvariable;
static void
myfunc(int idx);

File two.c:
static int myvariable;            /* no conflict with file one.c */
static int myfunc(int idx); /* no conflict */

The example of getch() and ungetch() in the previous section is one situation where static variables would constitute better design. The two functions would remain extern as they might be called from functions in other files, but the variables buffer and bufidx only require file-scope. Thus, static is to preferred over extern where possible as it permits more modular design. As a rule, and where possible, static functions are preferred over external functions, static variables are preferred over external variables, and local variables are preferred over static variables.

Aside. Many programs today operate using multiple *threads* of control, meaning that various parts of the program operate concurrently, or over a timeslice so as to appear concurrent. Extreme caution is required if using functions that rely on static or external variables in such programs. Temporal dependencies on the value of external variables may be violated as the different threads are switched in and out. In general, variables with static extent are best avoided in multi-threaded programs (unless they are explicitly synchronised).

## 1.    Scope Resolution and Name Hiding

It is possible for a program to have two variables of the same name with overlapping scope such that they are potentially visible from the same place. In such situations, one variable will hide the other. C specifies that the variable with more restricted scope will be visible, and the other hidden. In other words, the variable that is "more local" has dominant visibility. This situation is demonstrated in the following program.

```
1. #include <stdio.h>
2
3. int modify(int, int);
4
5. int x=1, y=3, z=5; /* external variables */
6
7 int main(void)
8       int x, z=0; /* local scope 1 */
9
10
11.       x = y + 1;
12.       while (x++ < 10) {
13.             int x, y = 0; /* local scope 2 */
14.             x = z % 5;
15.             printf("In loop \tx= °/,d\ty= °/,d\tz= °/,d\n", x, y+—+, z++);
16.       }
17
18.       printf ("Before modify()\tx= /d\ty= /d\tz= /d\n", x, y, z);
19.       z = modify(x, y);
20.       printf ("After modify()\tx= /d\ty= °/,d\tz= /d\n", x, y, z);
21. }
22
23. int modify(int a, int b)
24. {
25.       z += a + b;
26.       return z;
27. }
```

This program produces the following output.

| | $x$ | | $y$ | | $z$ | |
|---|---|---|---|---|---|---|
| In loop | $x$ | 0 | $y$ | 0 | $z$ | 0 |
| In loop | $x$ | 1 | $y$ | 0 | $z$ | 1 |

| | x | y | z |
|---|---|---|---|
| In loop | x = 2 | y = 0 | z = 2 |
| In loop | x = 3 | y = 0 | z = 3 |
| In loop | x = 4 | y | z = 4 |
| In loop | x = 0 | y = 0 | z = 5 |
| Before modify() | x = 1 | y = 3 | z = 6 |
| After modify() | x = 1 | y = 3 | z = 19 |

This output is a result of the C name-hiding rules. A brief discussion of the above example may help clarify their properties.

1. Identifier x refers to x-local-scope-1, and y to y-global-scope.

2. This line represents one of the more difficult instances of name-hiding: does x refer to the inner local block or the outer one? In fact, x refers to x-local-scope-1, not to x-local-scope-2, which is declared within the compound statement following the while, and is not in scope for the while conditional itself.

14-15 Identifiers x and y refer to the inner local-scope-2, and z refers to the outer local-scope-1.

18-20 Identifiers x and z refer to the outer local-scope-1, and y refers to the global-scope.

23-27 Identifiers a and b are local to the function block, while z is a global variable.

The problem of name hiding doesn't end there. Because C's scoping rules specify that the scope of an identifier begins at its point of declaration rather than the top of the block in which it is defined, a further non-intuitive name-hiding situation can occur. For example, consider the following code segment.

```
float i = 5.f;
{
    int i = i;
    int
```

$$i$$

$$=$$

$$\overline{0}$$

$$:$$

$$\}$$

Intuitively, one might think that j would be initialised by the inner-most i, the int. However, it turns out that int i does not exist until it is declared below j, so that j is initialised with the only i in scope at its declaration: float i = 5.f.

Name-hiding issues are easily avoided by defining appropriate variable names. It is bad practice to rely on the scope-resolution rules, and name-hiding leads to confusing and error-prone code. Avoid same-name identifiers for functions or variables that might share the same scope.

## 1. __Summary of Scope and Extent Rules__

Functions are extern by default, as are variables defined outside of any function. External functions and variables have *external* or *program scope,* which means they are visible across the entire (possible multi-file) program. Functions and external variables that are declared static have *file scope,* which means their visibility is limited to the source file in which they are defined. Variables defined within a function or block have *local scope,* and are not visible outside of their enclosing block even if declared static.

Functions and external variables have *static extent,* meaning that they are created before program execution and exist until the program terminates. Local variables declared static also have static extent. Non-static local variables have *local* or *automatic extent* and are destroyed when they go out-of-scope. Variables with static extent are initialised to zero by default, but variables with automatic extent are not given a default initial value.

In general, a variable can be defined with a storage class extern, static, or auto. The general form of a variable definition is as follows,

<storage class> <type qualifier> <type> <identifier> = <value> ;

where the assignment to an initial value is optional in general, but mandatory for variables qualified by const. For example,

static const double LightSpeed = 2.9979e8; / m/s */

Additional scope and extent identities. It is possible to define variables with *dynamic extent* such that their lifetime is managed explicitly by the programmer. Dynamic memory management is performed via the standard library functions malloc() and free(), and is discussed in Chapter 9.

Some other instances of scope are mentioned here for identifiers that are not functions or variables. Preprocessor macros (see Chapter 10) have file scope from the point they are defined to the bottom of the file (unless undefined by #undef). Named labels, such as used by goto (see Section 3.8), have function scope.

# 1. **Header Files**

Identifiers must the declared in a source file before they can be used. Rather than typing declarations explicitly in each source file that uses them, it is generally convenient to collect common declarations in *header files,* and include the relevant headers in the source files as required. Inclusion of header files is performed by the C preprocessor as specified by the #include directive.

> *The* #include *preprocessor command causes the entire contents of a specified source text file to be processed as if those contents had appeared in place of the* #include *command [HS95, page 53].*

Header files are used to store declarations shared over multiple source files including function prototypes, external variables, constants, macros, and user-defined data types. Collecting these declarations in header files avoids code duplication, and so avoids possible typographical errors and declaration mismatches. It also makes changes easier to enact as they only need to be made in one place.

Header file names are suffixed with .h by convention. The standard library headers are included using angle brackets to enclose the filename as follows.

    #include <filename.h>

Angle brackets indicate that the header file is located in some "standard" place according to the compiler-implementation search rules. Usually this means that the header is in the compiler search path. Header files from other libraries may also be included using the angle bracket syntax if they too reside on the compiler search path. A second form of include syntax uses double quotes,

    #include "filename.h"

which indicate that the header file is located in some "local" place, usually the current directory. The search for files included using the double-quote syntax begins in the local places and then looks in the standard places. The general intent of the " " form is to denote headers written by the application programmer, while the < > form indicates (usually standard) library headers.


## *1.* **Modular Programming: Multiple File Programs**

> *The functions and external variables that make up a C program need not all be compiled at the same time; the source text of the program may be kept in several files, and previously compiled routines may be loaded from libraries [KR88, page 80].*

Large-scale C programs are organised so that related functions and variables are grouped into separate source files. Grouping code by source file is central to C's compilation model, which compiles each file separately to produce individual object modules, and these are later linked to form the complete program. Separate compilation, in conjunction with the C scoping rules, gives rise to the paradigm of *modular programming.*

This code organisation strategy works as follows. Each source file is a module containing related functions and variables. The declarations of functions and variables (and constants and data-types) to be shared with other modules are stored in an associated header file; this is called the *public interface*. Access to the module from other modules is restricted to the public interface.

Functions defined in a module that are called only by other functions within that module are declared static. These functions comprise the *private interface*—functions visible only from within the module, as part of the module's internal implementation. Similarly, external variables used only within the module are declared static. These private interface declarations are not added to the header file, but are declared at the top of the source file.

The advantages of modular programming are as follows.

- Groups of related functions and variables are collected together. This leads to more intuitive use of a library of code than just a disorganised set of functions. Modules represent a higher level of abstraction than functions.

- Implementation details are hidden behind a public interface. This is useful for shielding users from complex algorithms or from non-portable code. Changes to the implementation can later be made without affecting client code (e.g., using a different algorithm, or porting platform- specific code to another platform). ˙

- Modules are decoupled from the rest of the program, allowing them to be built, tested, and debugged in isolation.

- Modules facilitate team program development where individuals can each work on different modules that make up the program.

It is difficult to state definitively the requirements for good modular design, but there are several rules-of-thumb that are generally applicable. First, it is desirable to minimise dependencies between modules. This involves, for example, minimising the use of external variables in the public interface, which tend to expose module implementation details and clutter the global namespace. Second, the public interface should be minimal; it should only contain functions required to use the module, not functions that are just part of the internal implementation. Similarly, variables, constants and data types that are not meant to be shared should not be part of the public interface, and should be declared in the source file, not the header file. Finally, it is good practice to restrict scope as much as possible, such that local variables are preferred over static variables which, in turn, are preferred over external variables, and static functions are preferred over external functions.

# Chapter 6

## Software Design

Software design is the process of decomposing a software problem into subsystems that interact to form a working whole. A well designed program is flexible, extensible and maintainable, and the key to such design is modularity. A modular design permits different parts of the program to be built and debugged in isolation. Thus, large-scale systems may be built without an overwhelming growth of complexity induced by dependencies between subtasks.

The process of software design usually involves a series of steps starting from stating the basic program requirements, and successively adding detail. A typical progression is as follows.

- Requirements and specification. The required program operation is described at a general and then a detailed level.

- Program flow. The flow of steps, decisions, and loops are planned, usually in the form of a diagram. This stage indicates dependencies between different subtasks. That is, it defines the sequence of operations, and the requirements for communication of data.

- Data structures. The format of variable types for passing data between functions must be chosen in order to design function interfaces.

- Top-down and/or bottom-up design. The structure and components of the program have to be designed. These two design paradigms facilitate organising overall structure and individual modules, respectively.

- Coding. Having produced a plan of how the program should appear, the problem becomes a matter of implementation. The process of coding often uncovers flaws in the original design, or suggests improvements or additional features. Thus, design and implementation tend to be iterative and not a linear progression.

- Testing and debugging. All non-trivial programs contain errors when first written, and should be subjected to thorough testing before being shipped to customers. Methods for systematic testing and debugging are beyond the scope of this text (for more information see, for example, [KP99, Ben00]).

It is important to realise that there are no hard-and-fast rules for good design. Software design is in part principles and formal methodologies, and in part an artform requiring experience and taste.

## 1.     Requirements and Specification

In order to write a program, it is first necessary to know what function the program is to perform. The first stage of design is to state a set of requirements, in general terms, for what the program is to do. For small projects, this might be sufficient and programming can commence immediately. However, for larger projects, these general requirements need to be refined into a more detailed specification.

A program specification is a more formal and detailed description of the program's operation. It defines particulars like input and output formats, responses to various events (such as user requests), and efficiency requirements. A specification may evolve during the program's implementation, as difficulties and new possibilities come to light. It is important to realise that design is an iterative process of refinement, not a linear progression from concept to code.

## 1.     **Program Flow and Data Structures**

Given a specification of the program's operation, it is a good idea to draw a diagram of the way the program will progress from initialisation to termination. Various formalisms exist for describing program flow, such as flow diagrams and state-transition diagrams. The key idea is to visualise how the program transitions from one state to another and what dependencies exist between different parts of the program.

Having defined dependencies, the variable types used to communicate data between different parts of the program should be specified. In addition to the basic types, C permits a programmer to create user-defined types of arbitrary complexity (using structs, for example), and these types are collectively termed *data-structures*? Following the definition of key data-structures, it becomes possible to start designing function interfaces.

## 1.     **Top-down and Bottom-up Design**

The top-down approach to design is to start with a set of high level tasks that will be called from main(), and recursively splitting each task into subtasks until a level of complexity is attained that permits the definition of reasonably simple function modules.

This idea of solving a problem by divide-and-conquer is illustrated in Figure 6.1, which shows a hierarchy where the higher-level functions are implemented in terms of the lower-level functions. Top-down design is useful for defining the overall structure of a program, and the dependencies between functions. Usually, the functions are first implemented as interfaces only, with do-nothing internals (also called "dummy" internals). This allows the program to run, albeit without any real utility, and individual functions can be written and tested within a working skeleton program. Thus, the entire program shell is laid out at the start, and the function internals are subsequently built and debugged one-at-a-time.

A key limitation of top-down design is that the resulting functions tend to be problem-specific (i.e., specific to the program at hand). They tend to be non-reusable, and the top-down design of each new project must start from scratch.

The bottom-up approach to software design is to identify various components that will be required by the program, and to build them in isolation from any design of the overall program structure. Assuming the appropriate argument types are known, the function interfaces can be designed, after which the internal implementations are usually straight-forward.

An advantage of bottom-up design is that the resulting modules are often more generic than those designed in a top-down approach. They tend to be less tied to the program at hand and more amenable to reuse. In the best-case, a bottom-up component can be designed even without knowledge of program dependencies; it is sufficient to just assume an interface and build an algorithm. Such

Figure 6.1: The top-down design approach. Starting from the highest level functions called from main(), recursively divide the program into sub-problems until the desired level of complexity is met. For example, the task of function f3() is implemented in part by the functions f3a() and f3b(), which each perform a particular subtask.

components form a library or toolbox of reusable modules that may be carried over from one project to the next. The C standard library is a good example of reusable bottom-up design.

The downside of bottom-up design is that it does not give a clear indication of how the individual program elements should be merged together. It does not present the "big picture", the overall structure of the program with its dependencies and function-call hierarchy. In addition, because components are developed in isolation, they often require the writing of *drivers* to permit testing and debugging. These drivers are small test programs that allow one to check the response of a component to various inputs. Writing drivers for a large number of different components can be a tedious process.

Top-down and bottom-up design are complementary, and practical design tends to use both strategies, working at both ends until they meet in the middle. Top-down design composes the overall program structure and call hierarchy, and bottom-up design builds key functionality and reusable components.

1.    **Pseudocode Design**

When designing the implementation of a particular function, it is sometimes helpful to write an outline of the algorithm at an abstract level in pseudocode rather than immediately writing C code. This form of function-level design concentrates on the algorithm structure without getting bogged down in syntactical details.

Pseudocode, also called *program design language,* is basically an English description of a code segment's intent. For example, consider the following pseudocode to get values from the user and compute their factorial.

loop number of times
    prompt user and get
    integer value calculate
    factorial print factorial

Given a pseudocode layout, it becomes straightforward to replace the pseudocode with C constructs. In sections where the code intent is not obvious, it is good practice to leave the original pseudocode in place as a comment.

# 1.     Case Study: A Tic-Tac-Toe Game

As an example of modular program design, this section presents the design and implementation of a simple game: Tic-Tac-Toe (also known as Noughts-And-Crosses). This program is simple enough to describe in a reasonable period of time, and complex enough to demonstrate the concepts required for larger-scale programs.

# 1.     Requirements

The aim of this program is to play a game of Tic-Tac-Toe against the computer. To begin, the user is welcomed to the game and asked if he wishes to have first go. The following game is turns-based, alternating between a request for the user's move, and the computer's own-move decision. After each turn, the result is printed in ASCII and, if there is a winner or a draw, the user is asked if he wishes to play again.

# 1.     Specification

The program is to print a welcome message to introduce the game and its rules.

Welcome to TIC-TAC-TOE.

The object of this game is to get a line of
X's before the computer gets a line of
O's. A line may be across, down, or
diagonal.

The board is labelled from 1 to 9 as follows:

1|2|3

4|5|6

7|8|9

This is followed by a request for whether the user wishes to start, with the integer 1 meaning 'yes' and 0 for 'no'.

Do you wish to go first (1-Yes, 0-No) ?

Each time the user is to make a move, a request is made for which location he wishes to choose, designated by a number between 1 and 9.

Your turn ( 1 - 9 ) :

After the user or the computer has made a decision, the resulting table is printed in ASCII. For example, after 5 turns, the board might look like

X| |

X|O|

|X|O

The game will terminate with a winner or a draw, and a comment is to be printed on account of the user's win, loss or draw, respectively.

> You win. Congratulations!!
> You lose. Better luck next time.
> Its a draw. How dull.

Finally, the user is asked if he wishes to play again and, if so, the game returns to the request of whether he wishes to have first go. Otherwise, the program terminates.

> Do you wish to play again (1-Yes, 0-No) ?

## 1. Program Flow and Data Structures

A rough sketch of the flow and dependencies of the program is shown in Figure 6.2. Such diagrams are very useful for getting an initial impression of modular composition and interaction. For small- scale projects, a simple hand-drawn diagram may be sufficient; for larger or team-built programs, they are typically precursors to more formal design diagrams. Figure 6.2 shows that there are a series of initialisation operations—a welcome screen and a prompt asking whether the users wants to go first—and then a main game-play loop. The game loop takes each player's decision in turn, prints the resulting game-board, and determines if the game continues or is over. On game-over, a message is printed based on the result (win, lose, or draw), and the user can choose to play again or quit.

The internals of this program are very simple, but it is necessary to specify the main variable types as they will affect the design of the function interfaces. From the flow diagram, it can be seen that there are three key data structures passed between the various functions. The first is the current state of the game for each of the nine locations on the Tic-Tac-Toe board. Each location may be in one of three states: empty, cross, or nought. It was decided to make the game states an integer array, and the possible states enumerated constants.

```
#define NUMSTATES 9
enum { NOTHING, CROSS, NOUGHT };
int state[NUMSTATES];
```

The other two data structures are the state of whose current turn it is (user or computer) and the state of the game result (still playing, user won, user lost, or draw). These variables were chosen to be enumerated types, and their possible states given by enumerated constants.

```
enum Turn { USER,
COMPUTER }; enum Result {
PLAYING, WIN, LOSE,
DRAW }; enum Turn turn;
enum Result result;
```

## 1. Bottom-Up Design

Looking at the program specifications, there are several functions that can be designed immediately without knowledge of the overall program structure. Consider the following examples.

All the input requirements for this program are solitary integers. Therefore it is worthwhile to write a function that extracts an integer from the keyboard input, and does appropriate input validation and error handling. This function would be passed a message string to prompt the user, and would return an integer.

```
int getint_from_user(char* message);
```

In the case of bad input, an error message would be printed and the prompt message reapplied.

Given that the current state of the game is stored in an integer array, a function can be built to print the output in ASCII. This function would have the following interface.

defining data-types, order of operations, key modules, and dependencies between modules.

```
void plot_state(int state[]);
```

We assume the number of states (9 for a 3x3 game) is known and defined by a symbolic constant, so it need not be passed as a function argument.

Another function dependent only on the current state of the game is the computer's decision making process. This function encapsulates the algorithm for choosing the computer's next move.

```
void get_computer_decision(int state[]);
```

The algorithm might be dumb, such as a random choice from the set of available locations, or smart, such as an exhaustive search of the game decision tree. Because the algorithm implementation is hidden, different algorithms can be trialed and debugged without change to the rest of the program.

Finally, another function well-suited to bottom-up design is the algorithm that determines whether the game is to continue playing, or if it has finished with a winner or a draw. This function requires only the current game state, but may be made more efficient if given the most-recent move as well. In the implementation shown, the current state and the most-recent player (user or computer) are passed.

```
enum Result compute_result(int state[], enum Turn turn);
```

1.     **Top-Down Design**

The structure of the program is refined by a top-down process, starting from the highest level functions called from main().

```
int main(void)
{
    enum Turn turn;
    enum Result result;
    int newgame = 1;
```

```
welcome();

while (newgame) {
    turn = who_goes_first();
    result = play_game(turn);
    gameover_message(result
    ); newgame =
    play_again();
};

goodbye(); return
0;
}
```

The choice of enumerated constants, and function and variable names makes the operation of main() quite clear, even without any comments. The functions all specify high-level operations and no low- level details are present to confuse the intent of the program. This approach greatly simplifies implementation changes and extensions. Implementation of these functions begins by writing all the definitions without any internals (except a return value, if required). Then the algorithms for each function are added and tested one-at-a-time.

The top-down heirarchy of this program is shown in Figure 6.3. All of the top-level functions are quite trivial, except for play_game(), which is split recursively into smaller subtasks. The structure obtained from this design meets with the bottom-up design of the various modules described previously, and turning the overall design into code from this point is straightforward.

Figure 6.3: The top-down design of the Tic-Tac-Toe program.


1.    **Benefits of Modular Design**

This design encloses each operation within a function. The function interfaces are minimal and decoupled, and completely hide any implementation details. The benefit of this modularity is that the code is flexible; changes and extensions are simple to implement.

Consider the following examples. One, it is possible to change the welcome and goodbye messages easily. Two, all input handling is encapsulated within the function getint_from_user(), which incorporates appropriate error checking. And three, if the game is ported to an environment with a graphical interface, only the input-output functions need to be revised.

By far the most technical part of this program was the computer decision-making function get_computer_decision(). To get the computer to make good choices is not trivial. However, to make the program run does not require an intelligent opponent, and a very simple random selection scheme was sufficient. Once the rest of the program was fully tested, it was straightforward to write cleverer decision-making code. This is a good example of hiding an algorithm behind an interface, allowing various implementations to be tested and compared without change to the rest of the program.

# Chapter 7

## Pointers

*A pointer is a variable that contains the address of a variable [KR88, page 93].*

Pointers provide a mechanism for the direct manipulation of memory. They are arguably the most powerful, and the most dangerous, feature of the C programming language. To the novice programmer who has not before encountered address-based computation, pointers can be a difficult concept to grasp. But with a little experience, they can be used to produce concise and efficient code.

*Pointers have been lumped with the goto statement as a marvelous way to create impossible- to-understand programs. This is certainly true when they are used carelessly, and it is easy to create pointers that point somewhere unexpected. With discipline, however, pointers can also be used to achieve clarity and simplicity [KR88, page 93].*

### 1.   What is a Pointer?

To explain the operation of a pointer, it is first necessary to understand, at least in a basic sense, the way in which memory is organised. Figure 7.1 shows a simplified picture of a layout of computer memory. A typical machine has an array of consecutively numbered memory cells. These numbers are termed *addresses*. Each cell consists of a set of bits, and the cell bit-pattern is the cell's *value.*

When a variable is defined, it is allocated a portion of memory. Thus, the variable has a value and an address for where that value resides. A pointer is a variable whose value is the address of another variable. Consider an example. (We will ignore, for the moment, various details such as the different byte-sizes for different types.) Let x be defined and initialised to the value 3.

    char x = 3;

Assume this variable is stored at address 62. A pointer px is subsequently defined, assume it is stored at address 25, and initialised with the address of x as follows.

    char *px = &x;

The value of px, therefore, is 62. Notice that a pointer is just another type of variable; it, also, has an address and may in turn be pointed-to by a pointer-to-a-pointer variable.

Memory cells may be grouped together to represent different variable types. On most machines, a cell is 8-bits long (i.e., one-byte). A char is usually one cell, a short int two cells, and a long int four cells. Each type (e.g., a double) has an associated pointer type (e.g., a double *), which is aware of the number of cells that the type occupies, and enables the compiler to behave appropriately with sequences of a particular type (e.g., an array of doubles).

On most machines, pointer variables also require multi-cell storage; typically for a 16-bit machine the pointer type is two-bytes, and for a 32-bit machine the pointer type is four-bytes. However, it is unwise to make assumptions about the size of a pointer type as such code is likely to be non-portable.

| 23 | 24 | 25 | 2 | 27 | | 6 |
|----|----|----|---|----|---|---|
|    |    | 6  |   |    | 61 | 2 |

| 54 | 14 | 62 | 2 | 45 | ... | 12 | 3 | 87 |
|----|----|----|---|----|-----|----|---|----|

I _____ 7

Figure 7.1: A simple memory model, where memory is an array of cells with consecutive addresses. At each address, a cell holds a particular value (i.e., bit-pattern). A variable x is defined that refers to the cell at address 62, and holds the value 3. A second variable px refers to the cell at address 25; it is defined as a pointer and holds the value 62, which is the address of x.

Aside. The one assumption about pointer sizes mandated by the C standard is that the pointer of type void* is large enough to store the value of any other pointer type. The void* pointer type is a special *generic object* pointer; it is designed to facilitate advanced techniques, which we examine in Chapter 14.

The size of a pointer type determines the maximum value it can represent, and hence the maximum range of addresses it can deal with. For example, a 16-bit pointer can only handle addresses between 0 and $2^{16} - 1$ (i.e., 65535). The main reason for the development of 32-bit machines was to enable greater memory addressing; a 32-bit pointer can address 0 to $2^{32} - 1$ (i.e., 4294967295) bytes of memory.

1.     **Pointer Syntax**

A pointer of a particular type is declared using the * symbol, and the address of a variable is obtained using the "address-of" operator &. For example,

```
int i;
int *j = &i;
```

defines a pointer-to-int variable j and initialises it with the address of i. This operation might equivalently have been written,

```
int *j, i;
j = &i;
```

It is worth noting that the * in a list of definitions refers only to the adjacent variable, and the spacing is irrelevant. For example, in the following,

```
int* i, j, * k;
```

i and k are pointers-to-int, while j is a plain int. The best style for such definitions is usually to place the * against the variable to which it refers.

```
int *i, *k, j;
```

The value of the variable to which a pointer points can be obtained using the *indirection* or *dereferencing* operator *.

```
int i = 2;
int *j = &i; /* Define a pointer-to-int j, and initialise with address of i. */ int x = *j;
/* x is assigned the value of i (that is, 2). */
```

The dereferencing use of * should not be confused with its use in pointer-declaration syntax. The declaration *, meaning "is a pointer-type variable" occurs only in variable or function declarations, and in all other circumstances the * means dereference or "access the pointed-to object".

Some examples of simple pointer operations are shown below.

```
char c = 'A';
char *pc = &c; /* pc points to c */
double d = 5.34; double *pd1, *pd2;

*pc  ='B'; /*  Dereferenced pointer: c is   now equal  to 'B'. */
pd1  =&d; /*   pd1 points to d */
pd2  =pd1; /*  pd2 and pd1 now both point  to d. */
*pd1 = *pd2 * 2.0; /* Equivalent to d = d * 2.0; */
```

Notice that pointers have different types specifying the type of object to which they can point. It is an error to assign a pointer to an object of a different type without an explicit cast.

```
float i = 2.f;
unsigned long *p1 = &i; /* Error: type mismatch, won't compile. */
unsigned long *p2 = (unsigned long *)&i; /* OK, but strange. */
```

The exception to this rule is the void* pointer which may be assigned to a pointer of any type without a cast.

It is dangerous practice to leave a pointer uninitialised, pointing to an arbitrary address. If a pointer is supposed to point nowhere, it should do so explicitly via the NULL pointer. NULL is a symbolic constant defined in the standard headers stdio.h and stddef.h. It is usually defined as

```
#define NULL ((void*) 0)
```

The constant values 0 or 0L may be used in place of NULL to specify a null-pointer value, but the symbolic constant is usually the more readable option.

Pointers may be declared const; and this may be done in one of two ways. The first, and most common, is to declare the pointer const so that the object to which it points cannot be changed.

```
int i = 5, j = 6; const int *p = &i;
*p = j; /* Invalid. Cannot change i via p. */
```

However, the pointer itself may be changed to point to another object.

```
int i = 5, j = 6; const int *p = &i;
p = &j;  /* Valid. p  now points to    j. */
*p = i;  /* Invalid.  Cannotchange  j via  p. */
```

The second form of const declaration specifies a pointer that may only refer to one fixed address. That is, the pointer value may not change, but the value of the object to which it points may change.

```
int i = 5, j = 6; int * const p = &i;
*p = j;   /* Valid. i   is now 6 */
p = &j;  /* Invalid.  p must always point   to i. */
```

It is possible to combine these two forms to define a non-changing pointer to a non-changeable object.

```
int i = 5, j = 6; const int * const p = &i;
*p = j; /* Invalid. i cannot be changed via p. */ p = &j; /* Invalid. p
must always point to i. */
```

- **Pass By Reference**

When a variable is passed to a function, it is *always* passed by value. That is, the variable is *copied* to the formal parameter of the function argument list. As a result, any changes made to the local variables within the function will not affect the variables of the calling function. For example, the following code to swap two variables will not work as intended.

```
swap(a, b); /* Pass values of a and b, respectively. */ void

swap(int x, int y)
/* x and y are copies of the passed arguments. */
{
    int tmp = x; /* The variable x is unrelated to the variable a */ x = y;
                 /* so this operation does not affect a. */
    y = tmp;
}
```

The variables x and y are different to a and b; they are stored at different addresses, and are simply initialised with the *values* of a and b.

The desired effect of this function can be achieved by using pointers. Pointers, as with any other variable, are passed by value, but their values are addresses which, when copied, still point to the original variables.

```
swap(&a, &b); /* Pass pointers to a and b, respectively. */

void swap(int* px, int* py)
/* px and py are copies of the passed pointer arguments. */
{
    int tmp = *px; /* The value of px is still the address of a */
    *px = *py;     /* so this dereferencing operation is equivalent to a = b. */
    *py = tmp;
}
```

Pointers provide *indirect* access to variables. This is why the * operator is called the *indirection* operator. Passing pointers as function arguments, therefore, is known as "pass-by-reference".

Pass by reference semantics is useful for implementing functions, such as swap() above, that require multiple return values. It is also useful as a mechanism to avoid copying large objects between functions; rather than make a copy of a large object, it is sufficient to pass a pointer to the object. (Arrays are a good example of this and, in C, arrays are passed by reference by default. When passed as a function argument, an array name is automatically converted to a pointer to its first element.) It is possible to prevent unwanted change to a pass-by-reference argument by declaring the parameter const. For example,

```
void cannot_change(const double *array, int len)
/* May perform read-only operations on array */
{
    int i;
    for (i = 0; i<len; ++i) {
        *(array + i) = 3.2; /* Invalid. Pointed-to objects cannot be changed. */
        array[i] =5.4;           /* Invalid. */
        printf("%f ", array[i]); /* Valid. */
    }
}
```

A const-pointer declaration has two purposes. It enables the compiler to enforce compile-time checks that the passed object is not changed within a function (i.e., it assists in ensuring the function is correct), and it informs the users of a function that the function will not modify the object they pass to it (i.e., it specifies a "non-modifying" guarantee).

• **Pointers and Arrays**

Pointers and arrays are strongly related; so much so that C programmers often assume they are the same thing. This is frequently the case, but not always. Whenever an array name appears in an expression, it is automatically converted to a pointer to its first element. For example,

```
unsigned buffer[256];
unsigned *pbuff1 = buffer;      /* Buffer  converted topointer,  &not  required. */
unsigned *pbuff2 = buffer +5;   /* A "pointer-plus-offset"expression. */
```

Here pbuff1 points to element 0 of the array, and pbuff2 points to element 5. Similarly, when an array name is passed to a function, it is converted to a pointer. Thus, in the following example, pdouble and darray are equivalent; they are both pointers.

```
void func(double *pdouble,   int  len);
void func(double darray[],    int  len);
```

An array name and a pointer to an array may be used interchangeably in many circumstances, such as array indexing. Consider the following example, where, within each commented group, the statements perform exactly the same operation.

```
char letters[26];

char *pc1 = letters; /* Equivalent pointer values. */
char *pc2 = &letters; char *pc3 = &letters[0];

letters[4] = 'e'; /* Equivalent indexes. */
pc1[4] = 'e';
*(letters +4) = 'e';
*(pc2 +4) = 'e';

pc3 = &letters[10]; /* Equivalent addresses. */ pc3 = &pc1[10]; pc3 = letters + 10; pc3 = pc2 + 10;
```

Notice that, for an array, its name (e.g., letters) when used in an expression is equivalent to its address (e.g., &letters), which is equal to the address of its first element (e.g., &letters[0]). The elements of an array can be accessed via the index operator (e.g., pc1[4]) or by a dereferenced pointer offset (e.g., *(pc2 + 4)). And the address of an array element can be obtained using the address-of operator (e.g., &letters[10]) or directly from the pointer offset (e.g., letters + 10).

However, an array is not equivalent to a pointer, and there are several important differences. First, an array is not a variable; its value cannot be changed.

```
int a1[10],
a2[10]; int *pa =
a1;

a1 = a2; /*
Error: won't
compile. */
```

```
a1++;    /* Error: won't compile. */
pa++;    /* Fine, a pointer is a variable. */
```

Second, an array name always refers to the beginning of a section of allocated memory, while a pointer may point anywhere at all (e.g., allocated memory, free memory, NULL). And third, the size of an array is the number of characters of memory allocated, while the size of a pointer is just the size of the pointer variable.

```
double
a1[10];
double *pa
= a1;
size_t s1 = sizeof(a1); /* s1 equals 10 * sizeof(double) */
size_t s2 = sizeof(pa); /* s2 equals sizeof(double *) */
```

- ## Pointer Arithmetic

Each variable type has a corresponding pointer type. This allows the compiler to automatically calculate the byte-offset required for indexing an array of that type. For example, on many machines a double is 8-bytes long; suppose a double-pointer pd has some initial value and is then incremented by one pd++. The address now held by pd is 8-bytes beyond the original address, so that it points to the next double. This mechanism makes pointer arithmetic simple and uniform for all types, and hides the details of type-sizes from the programmer.

So, in general, if p is a pointer to some element of an array, then p++ increments p to point to the next element, and p += n increments it point n elements beyond where it did originally. C permits a variety of arithmetic operations to be performed on pointer types as illustrated in the following example.

```
float fval, array[10]; float *p1, *p2, *p3 = &array[5]; int i=2, j; p1 = NULL; p2 = &fval; p1 = p2; p2 =
p3 - 4; p2 += i; j = p3 - p2; i = p2 < p3;
/* Assignment to NULL (or to 0 or 0L). */
/* Assignment to an address. */
/* Assignment to another pointer (of same type). */
*/
```

```
*/
/* Addition or subtraction by an integer: a pointer-offset expression. /* Another pointer-offset expression. */
/* Pointer subtraction: gives the number of elements between p2 and p3 /* Relational operations <, >, ==, !=, <=, >= */
```

At the end of the sequence of operations above, p1 points to the address of fval, p2 points to the fourth element of array, p3 points to the sixth element of array, i equals one, and j equals 2.

Integer arithmetic operations (i.e., pointer-offset expressions) permit access to array elements at some location relative to the current element. Relational comparisons (i.e., ==, <, >=, etc) are for determining whether the *position* of an array element is before or after another. And a numerical value for this relative position can be found by pointer subtraction.

Note. The arithmetic and relational operations are only valid for pointers to elements of the same array. Their behaviour is undefined if applied to pointers from different arrays.

The following arithmetic operations may not be applied to pointers. Addition or subtraction by a floating-point value, and multiplication or division by a value of any type. Assignment to any

non-pointer type is not permitted (although this can be forced using a cast). Also, while subtraction of two pointers is valid, addition of two pointers is not.

As an example of using pointer arithmetic in place of array indexing, consider the following implementations of strcpy(), a variant of the standard library function for copying a string t to a character array s. The first implementation uses array indexing.

```
void strcpy (char *s, char *t)
{
    int i=0;
    while ((s[i] = t[i]) != '\0')
        ++i;
}
```

Recall that an array index operation is equivalent to a dereferenced pointer offset (e.g., s[i] is equivalent to *(s+i)), so each iteration of the above loop involves three additions. The next implementation increments the pointers directly.

```
void strcpy (char *s, char *t)
{
    while ((*s = *t) != '\0') {
        ++s;
        ++t;
    }
}
```

This results in just two additions per loop. The final implementation below is a common variant of the second one. It neglects the explicit comparison with \0 (as the \0 character has value zero), and moves the increment operations inside the conditional expression. The loop will now terminate when the value of *s is 0.

```
void strcpy (char *s, char *t)
{
    while (*s++ = *t++)
        ;
}
```

This code is perhaps more cryptic to the novice than the previous implementations, but occurs often in C programs. Learning the idioms of experienced C programmers is part of the process of becoming a proficient C programmer.

Style note. The efficiency gains of pointers over array indexes is largely irrelevant with modern optimising compilers. For the above implementations of strcpy(), a good compiler would produce exactly the same executable code. It is usually bad practice to write obscure pointer-based code solely for the sake of efficiency; pointer arithmetic is best used when it makes code simpler and more readable.

A couple of lesser-known facts about pointers and arrays. First, an index can be negative so long as it still refers to an element within the array. For example,

```
int array[10]; int *pa = array + 5;
int i = pa[-3]; /* i equals the value of array[2] */
```

Second, the pointer one-past-the-end of an array is valid for pointer arithmetic.

```
int array[10];
int *pa, *end = &array[10];

for (pa = array; pa != end; ++pa)
    *pa = end - pa; /* Values of array elements will be: 10,9,8,7,6,...,1 */
```

However, this pointer may not be dereferenced. A pointer one-before-the-beginning of an array may not, in general, be used for pointer arithmetic; it is non-standard but works on many (perhaps most) machines.

```
int array[N];
int   *one_past1 = array + N;  /*  OK */
int   *one_past2 = &array[N]; /*  OK */
int   val1 = *(array + N);      /*  Undefined*/
int   val2 = array[N];          /*  Undefined*/
int *one_before = array - 1; /* Non-standard, but works on most platforms. */
```

Important. Pointer accesses outside of array bounds are not checked by the compiler. For example,

```
int array[10];
int *pa = array + 10;
int val = *++pa; /* Invalid, but will compile OK. */
```

Out-of-bounds accesses are arguably the greatest source of subtle runtime bugs, rivaled only by dynamic memory issues (such as memory-leaks or accessing deallocated memory). The problem with faulty pointer arithmetic is that the error might not have an obvious effect. In the best case, it might cause the program to crash immediately. More likely, the program will continue to run, may produce occasional weird results, and will crash unexpectedly at some critical moment (such as while demonstrating the program to a customer). It is imperative that pointers only access allocated memory regions, and that appropriate bounds checking is used to prevent access to invalid memory locations.

- **Return Values and Pointers**

A function may return a pointer. For example,

```
int* func_returns_pointer(void);
```

However, in many circumstances returning a pointer is a mistake and will not do what is expected. The problem arises if the object to which the pointer refers is local to the function. The local object will be destroyed when the function finishes, and the returned address will point to an invalid location. This error also applies to arrays defined within functions. In the following example,

```
int* misguided(void)
{
    int array[10], i; /* array has local extent: destroyed at end-of-block. */

    for (i = 0; i < 10; ++i) array[i] = i; return array;
}
```

the pointer to array ceases to refer to valid memory once array has been destroyed.

Returning pointers from functions is fine provided the object pointed-to remains in existence. Thus, it is valid to return a pointer to a static variable (which has static extent).

```
double* geometric_growth(void)
{
    static double grows =0.1; /* grows exists for lifetime of program. */
    grows *= 1.1; return &grows;
}
```

Similarly, variables with dynamic extent (i.e., variables allocated using malloc()) can be safely returned by a pointer. Pointers may also be returned if they refer to a function input argument which is itself a pointer. For example, a pointer might refer to an element within a passed array.

```
char* find_first(char* str, char c)
/* Return pointer to first occurrence of c in str. Return NULL if not found. */ {
    while(*str++ != '\0')
        if (*str == c) return
    str; return NULL;
}
```

- **Pointers to Pointers**

Sometimes it is desirable to pass a pointer to a function and to change the value of the pointer itself; that is, to change what it points to. This can be done using a pointer-to-a-pointer as in the following (rather contrived) example.

```
void func(int **pptr, int i, int j)
{
    if (i<j) *pptr = &i; else *pptr = &j;
}
```

This concept may be applied further, so that we can have a pointer-to-a-pointer-to-a-pointer, and so on. But such constructions are rarely necessary.

Changing the value of a pointer inside a function is just one application of pointers-to-pointers. More frequently they appear in relation to arrays of pointers, which are addressed in Section 8.4.

- **Function Pointers**

*In C, a function itself is not a variable, but it is possible to define pointers to functions, which can be assigned, placed in arrays, passed to functions, returned by functions, and so on [KR88, page 118].*

Function pointers are a very useful mechanism for selecting, substituting or grouping together functions of a particular form. For example, they may be used to pass functions as arguments to other functions. Or, they may be collected into an array of function pointers as a "dispatch table", where a certain function is invoked based on an array index.

The declaration of a function pointer must specify the number and type of the function arguments and the function return type. For example, the following declaration is a pointer to a function that has a double and an int argument and returns a double.

```
double (*pf)(double, int);
```

Thus, it is not possible to define a completely generic function pointer, only one that points to a certain category of function that fits the declaration.

Notice the use of parentheses around the identifier (*pf). This is necessary to distinguish a pointer-to-a-function from a function-that-returns-a-pointer.

```
int (*pf)(char); /* pointer-to-function: input char, return int */ int *f(char); /*
function: input char, return pointer-to-int */
```

In a function declaration, it is possible to declare a function pointer without using an identifier; (this is the case also with any other function argument).

```
void myfunc(char *, int, unsigned (*)(int));
```

However, it is usually better practice to include identifiers in function prototypes, as it improves readability.

```
void myfunc(char *message, int nloops, unsigned (*convert)(int));
```

The following example program uses function pointers to pass functions as arguments to another function. This allows the the latter function to perform a variety of operations without any change to its own algorithm. (Notice that, like arrays, function names are automatically converted to pointers without using the address-of operator &.)

```
#include <stdio.h>
#include <assert.h>

double add(double a,     double       b)      { return a + b; }
double sub(double a,     double       b)      { return a — b;      }
double mult(double a, double b) { return a * b; }
double div(double a, double b) { assert(b != 0.0);
return a / b; }

void execute_operation(double (*f)(double,double), double x, double y)
{
    double result = f(x,y);
    printf("Result of operation on %3.2f and %3.2f is %7.4f\n", x, y, result);
}

int main(void)
{
    double val1=4.3, val2=5.7; execute_operation(add,
    val1, val2); execute_operation(sub, val1, val2);
```

```
    execute_operation(mult, val1, val2);
    execute_operation(div, val1, val2);
}
```

Function pointers may be used to separate out certain sub-algorithm operations from within a general purpose main algorithm. This allows different sub-algorithms to be swapped in or out at run time. A common example is a generic sorting algorithm that uses function pointers to implement its sorting criterion.

```
void generic_sort(int *array, int len, int (*compare)(int, int));
```

```
int greater_than(int a, int b) { return a > b; } /* Possible sorting criterion. */
int less_than(int a, int b) { return a < b; } /* Possible sorting criterion. */
```

```
generic_sort(values, 20, less_than); /* Using the sort algorithm. */
```

## Chapter 8


## Arrays and Strings


An array is a group of variables of a particular type occupying a contiguous region of memory. In C, array elements are numbered from 0, so that an array of size N is indexed from 0 to $N-1$. An array must contain at least one element, and it is an error to define an empty array.

```
double empty[0]; /* Invalid. Won't compile. */
```

- ### Array Initialisation

As for any other type of variable, arrays may have local, external or static scope. Arrays with *static extent* have their elements initialised to zero by default, but arrays with local extent are not initialised by default, so their elements have arbitrary values.
It is possible to initialise an array explicitly when it is defined by using an initialiser list. This is a list of values of the appropriate type enclosed in braces and separated by commas. For example,

```
int days[12] = { 31, 28, 31, 30, 31, 30, 31, 31, 30, 31, 30, 31 };
```

If the number of values in the initialiser list is less than the size of the array, the remaining elements of the array are initialised to zero. Thus, to initialise the elements of an array with *local extent* to zero, it is sufficient to write

```
int localarray[SIZE] = {0};
```

It is an error to have *more* initialisers than the size of the array.
If the size of an array with an initialiser list is not specified, the array will automatically be allocated memory to match the number of elements in the list. For example,

```
int days[] = { 31, 28, 31, 30, 31, 30, 31, 31, 30, 31, 30, 31 };
```

the size of this array will be twelve. The size of an array may be computed via the sizeof operator,

```
int size = sizeof(days); /* size equals 12 * sizeof(int) */
```
which returns the number of *characters* of memory allocated for the array. A common C idiom is to use sizeof to determine the number of elements in an array as in the following example.

```
nelems = sizeof(days) / sizeof(days[0]); for(i = 0; i<nelems; ++i)
    printf("Month %d has %d days.\n", i+1, days[i]);
```
This idiom is invariant to changes in the array size, and computes the correct number of elements even if the type of the array changes.[1] For this reason, an expression of the form

```
sizeof(array) / sizeof(array[0])
```

is preferred over, for example,

```
sizeof(array) / sizeof(int)
```

as array might one day become an array of type unsigned long.

Note. sizeof will only return the size of an array if it refers to the original array name. An array name is automatically converted to a pointer in an expression, so that any other reference to the array will not be an array name but a pointer. For example,

```
int *pdays = days;
int  size1 = sizeof(days);      /*   size1 equals   12 * sizeof(int) */
int  size2 = sizeof(days + 1);  /*   size2 equals   sizeof(int  *) */
int  size3 = sizeof(pdays);     /*   size3 equals   sizeof(int  *) */
```
Similarly, if an array is passed to a function, it is converted to a pointer.

```
int count_days(int days[], int len)
{
    int total=0;
    /* assert will fail: sizeof(days) equals sizeof(int *) and len equals 12 */
    assert(sizeof(days) / sizeof(days[0]) == len); while(len—)
        total += days[len];
    return total;
}
```

1.   **Character Arrays and Strings**

Character arrays are special. They have certain initialisation properties not shared with other array types because of their relationship with strings. Of course, character arrays can be initialised in the normal way using an initialiser list.

```
char letters[] = { 'a', 'b', 'c', 'd', 'e' };
```

But they may also be initialised using a string constant, as follows.

```
char letters[] = "abcde";
```
The string initialisation automatically appends a \0 character, so the above array is of size 6, not 5. It is equivalent to writing,

```
char letters[] = { 'a', 'b', 'c', 'd', 'e', '\0' };
```

Thus, writing

```
char letters[5] = "abcde"; /* OK but bad style. */
```
while not an error, is very poor style, as the size of the array is too small for its initialiser list.

An important property of string constants is that they are allocated memory; they have an address and may be referred to by a char * pointer. For constants of any other type, it is not possible to assign a pointer because these constants are not stored in memory and do not have an address. So the following code is incorrect.

```
double *pval = 9.6;          /* Invalid. Won't compile. */
int *parray = { 1, 2, 3 }; /* Invalid. Won't compile. */
```

However, it is perfectly valid for a character pointer to be assigned to a string constant.

```
char *str = "Hello World!\n"; /* Correct. But array is read-only. */
```

This is because a string constant has static extent—memory is allocated for the array before the program begins execution, and exists until program termination—and a string constant expression returns a pointer to the beginning of this array.

Note. A string constant is a constant array; the memory of the array is read-only. The result of attempting to change the value of an element of a string constant is undefined. For example,

```
char *str = "This is a string constant";
str[11] = 'p'; /* Undefined behaviour. */
```

The static extent of string constants leads to the possibility of various unusual code constructs. For example, it is legitimate for a function to return a pointer to a string constant; the string is not destroyed at the end of the function block.

```
char * getHello()
/* Return a pointer to an array defined within the function */
{
    char *phello = "Hello World\n";
    return phello;
}
```

It is also valid to directly index a string constant, as demonstrated in the following function, which converts a decimal value to a value in base b, and, for bases 11 to 36, correctly substitutes letters for digits where required.

```
void print_base_b (unsigned x, unsigned b)
/* Convert decimal value x to a representation in base b. */
{
    char buf[BUF_SIZE]; int q=x, i=0; assert(b >=
    2);

    /* Calculate digit for each place in base b */ do {
        assert(i <
        BUF_SIZE); x =
        q; q = x/b;
        buf[H—+] =
    "0123456789abcdefghijklmnopqrstuvwxyz" [x — q*b];
    } while (q>0);

    /* Print digits, in reverse order (most-significant place first) */
```

```
        for ( --i; i>=0; --i)
                printf("%c",
        buf[i]); printf
        ("\n");
}
```

So, for a pointer to a string constant, the string constant is read-only. However, for a character *array* initialised by a string constant, the result is read-writable. This is because, with an array definition, the compiler first allocates memory for the character array and then *copies* the elements of the string constant into this memory region. Note, the *only* time a string is copied automatically by the compiler is when a char array is initialised. In every other situation, a string has to be manually copied character-by-character (or by functions such as strcpy() or memcpy()).

A collection of valid operations on various array types is shown below.

```
short val = 9;
short *pval = &val;              /* OK */
double array[] = {1.0, 2.0, 3.0 }; double
*parray = array;                 /* OK
*/
char str[] = "Hello World!\n"; /* Correct. Array is read-write. */ str[1]
= 'a';                           /* OK */
```

1.   **Strings and the Standard Library**

The standard library contains many functions for manipulating strings, most of which are declared in the header-file string.h. This section describes several of the more commonly-used functions.

- size_t strlen(const char *s). Returns the number of characters in string s, excluding the terminating '\0' character. The special unsigned type size_t is used instead of plain int to cater for the possibility of arrays that are longer than the maximum representable int.

- char *strcpy(char *s, const char *t). Copies the string t into character array s, and returns a pointer to s.

- int strcmp(const char *s, const char *t). Performs a lexicographical comparison of strings s and t, and returns a negative value if s < t, a positive value if s > t, and zero if
  s == t.

- char *strcat(char *s, const char *t). Concatenates the string t onto the end of string s. The first character of t overwrites the '\0' character at the end of s.

- char *strchr(const char *s, int c). Returns a pointer to the first occurrence of character c in string s. If c is not present, then NULL is returned.

- char *strrchr(const char *s, int c). Performs the same task as strchr() but starting from the reverse end of s.

- char *strstr(const char *s, const char *t). Searches for the first occurrence of substring t in string s. If found, it returns a pointer to the beginning of the substring in s, otherwise it returns NULL.

The functions strncpy(), strncmp(), and strncat() perform the same tasks as their counterparts strcpy(), strcmp(), and strcat(), respectively, but include an extra argument n, which limits their operations to the first n characters of the right-hand string.

A standard function that can perform the operations of both strcpy() and strcat(), and even more, is sprintf(). It is a general purpose string formatting function that behaves identically to printf(), but copies the resulting formatted string to a character array rather than sending it to stdout. sprintf() is a very versatile string manipulation function.

Aside. In general, the concatenation of two strings requires the use of a function like strcat(). However, string *constants* may be concatenated at compile time by placing them adjacent to one another. For example, "this is " "a string" is equivalent to "this is a string". Compiletime concatenation is useful for writing long strings, since typing a multi-line string constant like

"this is
        a string"

is an error. An alternative way to write multi-line string constants is to write

"this is \ a
string"

where the first character of the second half of the string occurs in the first column of the next line without preceding white-space. (This is one occasion where white-space matters in a C program.) Usually the adjacency method is preferred over the '\' method.

1.    **Arrays of Pointers**

Since pointers are themselves variables, they can be stored in arrays just as other variables can. For example, an array of N pointers to ints has the following syntax.

    int *parray[N];

Each pointer in an array of pointers behaves as any ordinary pointer would. They might point to an object, to NULL, to an illegal memory location, or to an array.

    double val = 9.7;
    double array[] = { 3.2, 4.3, 5.4 }; double
    *pa[] = { &val, array+1, NULL };

In the above example, element pa[i] is a pointer to a double, and *pa[i] is the double variable that it points to. The dereferenced *pa[0] is equal to 9.7, and *pa[1] is 4.3, but pa[2] is equal to NULL and may not be dereferenced.

    int a1[] = { 1, 2, 3, 4 }; int a2[] = { 5, 6, 7 };
    int *pa[] = { a1, a2 }; /* pa stores pointers to beginning of int **pp = pa; /* Pointer-to-a-pointer holds
    address int *p = pa[1]; /* Pointer to the second array in pa. int val;
    each array. */ of beginning of */
    pª.
    */

If an element in an array of pointers also points to an array, the elements of the pointed-to array may be accessed in a variety of different ways. Consider the following example.

    val = pa[1][1]; /* equivalent operations: val = 6 */
    val = pp[1][1];
    val = *(pa[1] + 1);
    val = *(pp[1] + 1);
    val = *(*(pp+1) + 1));

val = p[1];

Notice that in an expression pa and pp are equivalent, but the difference is that pa is an array name and pp is a pointer. That is, pp is a variable and pa is not.

Arrays of pointers are useful for grouping related pointers together. Typically these are one of three types: pointers to large objects (such as structs), pointers to arrays, or pointers to functions.

For the first two categories, most interesting applications of pointer arrays involve the use of dynamic memory, which is discussed in Chapter 9. However, a simple example of an array of pointers to arrays is the following program which obtains a number from the user and prints the name of the corresponding month.

```c
#include <stdio.h>

int main(void)
{
        char *months[] = { "Illegal", "January", "February",
                "March", "April", "May", "June", "July",
                "August", "September", "October", "November",
                "December" };
        int i, j;

        printf("Input an integer between 1 and 12: ");
        scanf("%d", &i); if (i<1 || i>12) i=0;

        printf ("Month number %d is %s.\n", i, months[i]); /*

        print string */ printf("The letters of the month are: ");
        for (j = 0; months[i][j] != '\0'; ++j) /* access elements
                using [][] */ printf("%c ", months[i][j]);
}
```

A common application for an array of function pointers is the construction of a "dispatch" table, which is used to invoke a particular function depending on the value of an array index. Each function in the array must have the same interface. The following example shows the syntax for defining an array of function pointers.

```c
int (*pf[10])(char *);
```

This statement defines a variable Pf, which is an array of pointers to functions where each function fits the interface specification: takes a char * argument and returns an int.

The example program below shows the use of an array of function pointers to perform simple arithmetic operations. Each function has the interface signature of two double arguments and returns a double.

```c
#include
<stdio.h>
#include
<assert.h>

double add(double a, double b) { return a
+ b; } double sub(double a, double b) {
return a — b; } double mult(double a,
double b) { return a * b; } double
```

```
div(double a, double b) { assert(b !=
0.0); return a / b; }

int main(void)
{
    int i;
    double val1, val2;
    double (*pf[])(double,double) = { add, sub, mult, div };

    printf ("Enter two floating-point values, and an integer
    between 0 and 3: "); scanf("%lf%lf%d", &val1, &val2, &i); if
    (i<0 || i>3) i = 0;

    printf ("Performing operation %d on %3.2f and %3.2f equals
    %3.2f\n", i, val1, val2, pf[i](val1, val2));
```

The declaration syntax for function pointers and arrays of function pointers rapidly becomes very complicated. A good mechanism for simplifying declarations is to break them up using typedef. The keyword typedef is used for creating new data-type names. For example, in the following declaration,

```
typedef char * String;
```

the name String becomes a synonym for char *, and can be used to define variables of this type.

```
String message = "This is a string.";
```

With regard to complicated function pointer declarations, different parts of the declaration can be given a name using typedef, so that the combined whole is more readable. For example, the declaration in the program above can be rewritten as

```
typedef double (*Arithmetic)(double,double);
Arithmetic pf[] = { add, sub, mult, div };
```

The name Arithmetic becomes a synonym for a function pointer of the specified type, and defining an array of such function pointers is simple. We discuss further uses of typedef in Sections 11.5 and 14.1.


## 1.    Multi-dimensional Arrays

*C provides rectangular multi-dimensional arrays, although in practice they are much less used than arrays of pointers [KR88, page 110].*

A multi-dimensional array is defined using multiple adjacent square brackets, and the elements of the array may be initialised with values enclosed in curly braces, as in the following example.

```
float   matrix[3][4] = {
           { 2.4,  8.7,  9.5, 2.3 },
           { 6.2,  4.8,  5.1, 8.9 },
           { 7.2,  1.6,  4.4, 3.6 }
};
```

The braces of the initialisation list are nested such that the inner braces enclose each row of the twodimensional array. In memory, a multi-dimensional array is laid out row-wise as a single dimensional array. For example, the layout in memory of matrix is equivalent to the following 1-D array.

```
float oneD[] = { 2.4, 8.7, 9.5, 2.3, 6.2, 4.8, 5.1, 8.9, 7.2, 1.6, 4.4, 3.6 };
```

As for one dimensional arrays, multi-dimensional arrays may be defined without a specific size. However, only the left-most subscript (i.e., the number of rows) is free, and the other dimensions must be given a definite value. For example,

```
float matrix[][4] = {          /* The 4 must be specified. */
       { 2.4, 8.7, 9.5, 2.3 },
       { 6.2, 4.8, 5.1, 8.9 }
};
```

To access an element of a multi-dimensional array, the correct notation is to enclose each subscript in a separate pair of square braces. This differs from many other programming languages, which use comma separated subscripts.

```
float a = matrix[1][2]; /* Correct. */
float b = matrix[1,2]; /* Wrong. */
void multiply(int (*r)[SIZE], const int a[][SIZE], const int b[SIZE][SIZE])
/* Multiply two (SIZE by SIZE) matrices, a and b, and store result in r.
 * The result matrix, r, must be zeroed before-hand. */
{
       int i, j, k;
= 0; i<SIZE; ++i)
for (j = 0; j<SIZE; ++j)
                    for (k = 0; k<SIZE; ++k)
                              r[i][j] += a[i][k] * b[k][j];
```

A multi-dimensional array may have any number of dimensions, and higher-dimensional initialiser lists involve a deeper level of nested braces for each dimension. The following example illustrates the general format.

```
short array3d[4][2][3] = {
       { {  0,  1,   2 },  { 3, 4,   5 } },
       { {  6,  7,   8 },  { 9, 10,  11 } },
       { { 12, 13,  14 },  { 15, 16,  17 } },
       { { 18, 19,  20 },  { 21, 22,  23 } }
};
```

Note, the above array may have been defined with the left-most subscript unspecified,

```
short array3d[][2][3] = ... ;
```

but the other dimensions must be fully qualified.

An example program using multi-dimensional arrays is given below. This program defines a two-dimensional array to represent a 3-by-3 matrix and passes it to a function which computes the product of two matrices.

```
#include <stdio.h> #define SIZE 3
for (i
}
int main(void)
{
int m1[][SIZE] = { { 1, 2, 3 },
                                                         { 4, 5, 6 },
                                                         { 7, 8, 9 }
};
int m2[SIZE][SIZE] = {0}; int i, j;
       multiply(m2, m1, m1); for (i=0; i<SIZE; ++i) {
              for (j=0; j<SIZE; ++j)
```

```
                        printf("%,3d ", m2[i][j]); printf ("\n");
        }
    }
```

The output for this program is the square of matrix m1.

```
    30   36   42
    66   81   96
   102 126 150
```

Notice, on line 5, the function interface for multiply() shows three equivalent declarations: a pointer to an array, a 2-D array with an unspecified left subscript, and a fully specified 2-D array, respectively. Notice that the pointer to an array is required to specify the size of the nonleft-most subscript. In addition, notice the parentheses about the *pointer-to-an-array* identifier, int (*r)[SIZE], this is to distinguish it from an *array-of-pointers,* int *r[SIZE].

Often multi-dimensional arrays and arrays of pointers may be used in an identical fashion. This can be a source of confusion to novice C programmers. For example, given the following array definitions,

```
char a[]   =  {1, 2, 3};
char b[]   =  {4, 5, 6};
char *c[] = { a, b };
char d[][3] = {{ 1, 2, 3 }, { 4, 5, 6 }};
```

The subscripts c[i][j] and d[i][j] will give the same results.

However, multi-dimensional arrays and arrays of pointers are different in both their representation and application. First, a multi-dimensional array occupies a single contiguous region of memory, while an array-of-pointers may point to disparate memory locations. Second, a multi-dimensional array is rectangular—each row is the same length, while an array of pointers may refer to arrays of different length (including nothing, NULL). Finally, a multi-dimensional array requires all but the left-most subscript to be specified when it is passed to function, while an array of pointers makes no such requirement.

In summation, arrays of pointers are usually the more flexible (and often more efficient) option, and so are used far more frequently than multi-dimensional arrays.

# Chapter 9

# Dynamic Memory

Often a program cannot know in advance how much memory it will require. Setting aside "enough" memory, such as defining a char array of sufficient size to hold the largest permitted string, is not convenient in many situations and may be difficult to manage.

Dynamic memory facilitates memory on demand. Memory is requested at runtime as required, and the lifetime of each memory allocation is controlled directly by the programmer.

# 1.  **Different Memory Areas in C**

C has four distinct areas of memory: the constant data area, the static-extent data area, the stack, and the heap. The first of these stores string constants and other data whose values are known at compile time. This area of memory is read-only, and the results of trying to modify it are undefined. The second data area is for variables that are defined extern or static, and so exist for the lifetime of the program. These variables are read-writable. Both of the first two memory areas are allocated when the program begins and destroyed when it terminates, and are managed by the compiler.

The memory area known as the *stack* is used to store local variables (i.e., variables with automatic extent). A local variable is allocated memory at the point where it is defined and this memory is released immediately as the variable goes out-of-scope. The stack behaves like a last-in-first-out (LIFO) queue. When variables are defined, they are "pushed onto the stack", and the stack-size increases. And at the end of a block, if several variables go out-of-scope at once, the variables are destroyed, or "popped off the stack", in reverse order to their allocation. Stack memory allocation is managed entirely by the compiler.

The *heap* memory area is for dynamically allocated storage and is managed, not by the compiler, but explicitly by the programmer. Requests for memory, and its subsequent destruction, are performed via a set of standard library functions, and the programmer has complete control over the lifetime of an allocated memory block. The flexibility and control provided by heap-allocated memory comes at the price of added responsibility on behalf of the programmer. The compiler does not check that the memory is managed correctly, and dynamic memory errors are a plentiful source of subtle runtime bugs.

It is worth noting that stack memory allocation is generally much faster than heap memory allocation, as stack allocation involves only an increment of the stack pointer, while heap allocation involves much more complex operations. For this reason, stack allocation is often preferred over heap allocation even at the cost of some wasted storage space. For example, an over-size char array, allocated on the stack, is often used to perform string operations rather than an exact-size array created on demand on the heap.

# 1.  **Standard Memory Allocation Functions**

The two key standard library functions for dynamic memory allocation and de-allocation, respectively, are malloc() and free(). The first, malloc() has the following interface,

    void *malloc(size_t size)

where size is the number of bytes of memory to allocate, and the return value is a pointer to this requested memory. Notice that the returned pointer is of type void*, which specifies a *generic pointer*, and can represent a pointer of any type. For example, to create an array of 10 integers, one writes

    int *p = malloc(10 * sizeof(int)); /* allocate bytes for 10 integers */

and the return value of malloc() is automatically converted to type int *. It is common to write an explicit cast to the desired type so as to clarify intent.

    int *p = (int *) malloc(10 * sizeof(int));

Typically requests for memory using malloc() will succeed, and the returned pointer points to a valid memory location. However, it is possible for the request to fail (e.g., if the available heap- space is full; a rare event on modern machines, but still possible), and when this happens malloc() returns a NULL pointer. It is important to always check the return value of malloc() for NULL so as to prevent invalid attempts to dereference the NULL pointer.

The de-allocation function free() releases memory allocated by malloc(), and returns it to the heap. It has the following interface,

    void free(void *)

and is used as follows (continuing from the previous example).

    free(p);

The conversion of a pointer of type int* to a pointer of type void* does not require an explicit cast (in C or C++), and so casts of this variety never appear in practice.

There are two other dynamic allocation functions in the C standard library, calloc() and realloc(). The first, calloc(), behaves almost the same as malloc() but, where malloc() returns a block of memory that is uninitialised (i.e., the cells contain arbitrary values), calloc() initialises the block with zeros. The interface for calloc() is slightly different to malloc() as it take two arguments

    void *calloc(size_t n, size_t size)

where the first specifies the number of objects in the requested array, and the second specifies the size of the object type. For example, the following statement allocates an array of 10 integers initialised to zero.

    int *p = calloc(10, sizeof(int)); /* allocate array of 10 integers, all 0 */

As for malloc(), calloc() returns NULL if the memory request fails.

The final memory allocation function, realloc(), is used to change the size of an existing block of dynamically allocated memory. That is, given a block of memory allocated by malloc(), calloc(), or realloc() itself, realloc() will adjust the size of the allocated memory to the new requested size. The interface of realloc() is as follows

    void *realloc(void *p, size_t size)

where p is a pointer to the current block of memory and size is the new requested size. The return value is a pointer to the resized memory block, or NULL if the request fails. Also, if realloc() is passed a size request of 0, then the memory pointed to by p is released, and realloc() returns NULL. In this case NULL does not indicate failure.

Calling realloc() does not change the existing *contents* of a memory block. If the block is reduced, then the excess cells are truncated and the values of the remaining cells are left unchanged. If, on the other hand, the block is increased, the old values are retained and the new cells will contain uninitialised (i.e., arbitrary) values. The action of realloc() is to grow or shrink a region of memory. If this can be done in-place, then realloc() might simply adjust certain bounds records and return but, if there is insufficient space in the current region within the heap, then realloc() will allocate a new block of memory of the appropriate size, copy across the values of the previous block, and release the old block. These operations are managed internally by realloc(), but they may affect application code if it has pointers into the old memory block; these pointers will be invalid if the block is copied elsewhere.

## 1. **Dynamic Memory Management**

Dynamic memory management is the responsibility of the application programmer, with virtually no help from the compiler. The programmer must keep track of various quantities such as object lifetimes, pointers to different memory locations, lengths of arrays, and so forth. Without good coding practices and careful implementation, dynamic memory can be a rich source of runtime errors which are often notoriously difficult to debug.

Consider, for example, the following function, which makes a copy of the string passed to it and returns a pointer to the copy.

```
char *string_duplicate(char *s)
/* Dynamically allocate a copy of a string. User must remember to
free this memory. */ {
    char *p = malloc(strlen(s) + 1); /* +1 for
    \0' */ return strcpy(p, s);
}
```

Notice that using dynamic allocation allows us to allocate exactly the right amount of memory to contain the string. The expression strlen(s)+1 is a common idiom for this operation with +1 to cater for the '\0' character. Notice, also, that the return value of strcpy() makes for a convenient return of the copy. However, this function is flawed because it fails to check the return value of malloc(), which, if NULL, will crash the program during the copy operation. A corrected version, adapted from [KR88, page 143], is shown below.

```
char *string_duplicate(char *s)
/* Dynamically allocate a copy of a string. User must remember to
free this memory. */ {
    char *p;

    p = (char *) malloc(strlen(s) + 1); /* +1 for
    \0' */ if (p != NULL)
        strcpy(p, s);
    return p;
}

    char s;
    s = string_duplicate("this is a string");

    free(s); /* Calling function must remember to free s. */
```

Neglecting the free(s) statement means that the memory is not released even when s goes out-ofscope, after which the memory becomes non-recoverable. This sort of error is known as a "memory leak", and can accumulate large quantities of dead memory if the program runs for a long period of time or allocates large data-structures.

Some common errors related to dynamic memory management are listed below.

- Dereferencing a pointer with an invalid address. If a pointer is not initialised when it is defined, it will contain an arbitrary value, such that it points to an arbitrary memory location. The result of dereferencing this pointer will depend on where it points (e.g., no effect, intermittent strange values, or program crash). Writing to memory via an invalid pointer is known as "memory corruption".

- Dereferencing a pointer that has been freed. This is a special case of the previous error. Once a memory block is released by calling free(p), the pointer p is no longer valid, and should not be dereferenced.

- Dereferencing a NULL pointer. This typically occurs because a system function returns NULL to indicate a problem and the calling function fails to implement appropriate checking. (For many compilers, dereferencing a NULL pointer is a simple bug to find as it causes the program to crash immediately, but this behaviour is not standard.)

- Freeing memory that has already been freed. Passing a previously freed pointer to free() will cause the function to dereference an invalid address.

- Freeing a pointer to memory that was not dynamically allocated. Memory that is not allocated on the heap, but on the stack or constant data area, say, cannot be released by free(). Attempting to do so will have undefined results.

- Failing to free dynamically allocated memory. Dynamic memory exists until it is explicitly released by free(). Failing to do so results in a "memory leak".

- Attempting to access memory beyond the bounds of the allocated block. Out-of-bounds errors occur if arrays are not properly bounds checked. A particularly common problem is the "off- by-one" array indexing error, which attempts to access elements one-before-the-beginning or one-past-the-end of an array, due to indexing arithmetic being not quite correct.

Good programming practices exist avoid these memory management errors, and following these rules will greatly reduce the risk of dynamic memory related bugs.

- Every malloc() should have an associated free(). To avoid memory leaks and memory corruption, there should be a one-to-one mapping of calls to malloc() and calls to free(). Preferably the call to free() should appear in the same function as the call to malloc() (rather than have one function return a pointer to dynamically allocated memory and expect the calling function to release it). Alternatively, one might write a create() function that allocates memory for an object and a companion destroy() function that frees it.

- Pointers should be initialised when defined. A pointer should never hold an arbitrary value, but should be initialised with either a valid address or NULL, which explicitly marks a pointer as "points nowhere".
    free(p); p = NULL;

    free(p); / OK, no effect. */


1.    **Example: Matrices**

This section presents a more complex example of dynamic memory, which involves functions for creating and destroying matrices. In Section 8.5, an example program shows the creation and use of a fixed-size (3 x 3) matrix, and the matrices created in the following example may be used similarly. The advantage of dynamic memory allocation is that the matrix sizes need not be known in advanced, and can be specified at run time.
    The first function allocates memory for a matrix with m rows and n columns. It is created as an array of m pointers, where each pointer points to a row of n elements.


```
double create_matrix(int m, int n)
/* Dynamically allocate an (m x n) matrix. Returns a pointer
to the beginning * of the matrix. This function does not check
                            for memory-allocation errors. */
{
        double
        **p; int
        i;

        p = (double **)malloc(m *
        sizeof(double *)); for (i = 0; i < m;
        ++i)
```

```
        p[i] = (double *)malloc(n * sizeof
(double)); return p;
}
```

The function return value is a pointer-to-a-pointer, so that the matrix elements may be accessed using multi-dimensional array notation as follows.

```
double **matrix = create_matrix(2,3);
matrix[0][2] = 5.4;
```

Notice that pointers referring to dynamically allocated memory may be safely returned by a function, as the memory continues to be valid until explicitly destroyed.

The above function will operate correctly unless malloc() returns NULL. Careless function design like this is an all-to-common programming practice and, if malloc() is unable to satisfy the request for more memory, the program will crash. A function that performs appropriate error checking, and returns NULL if malloc() fails, is shown below.

```
1.      for (i = 0; i < m; ++i) {
2.          p[i] = (double *)malloc(n * sizeof(double));
3.          if (p[i] == NULL)
4.              goto failed;
5.      }
6.      returnp;
```
20
```
1.      /* Allocation failed, delete already allocated memory. */
2.  failed:
3.      for ( -i; i >= 0; --i)
4.              free(p[i]);
5.      free(p);
6.      returnNULL;
7. }
```

7 The assert() checks for logical errors in the program. Specifically, that the calling function does not request matrices of zero or negative size.

10-11 The first memory allocation is the the array of m pointers. If this fails, there is nothing left to do, and the program simply returns NULL.

14-19 The next set of allocations are for each row of the matrix. If any one of these allocations fails, the previous successful allocations must be released before the function returns so as to prevent memory leaks. In the event of an error, the program jumps out of the allocation loop to the error-handling code. This jump demonstrates another legitimate use of goto, which permits simpler code than would be possible without it.

22-26 The error-handling code first loops through each successfully allocated matrix row and frees them. It then frees the array of pointers. It is critical that deallocation is performed in this order as the row pointers would be invalid if the pointer array was freed first.

The next function is a companion to create_matrix(), which performs appropriate deallocation operations to release the memory representing a matrix object. This function takes as arguments a pointer-to-a-pointer reference to the matrix, and the matrix dimensions m and n. It is important that the same dimensions are passed for the matrix destruction as for its creation, otherwise it will not be released correctly.

```c
1.  void destroy_matrix(double **p, int m, int n)
2.  /* Destroy an (m x n) matrix. Notice, the n variable
3.   * is not used, it is just there to assist
using the function. */ 4 {
4.      int i;
5.      assert(m>0  && n>0);
7
1.      for (i = 0; i < m; ++i)
2.          free(p[i]);
3.      free(p);
4.  }
5.  double **create_matrix(int m, int n)
6.  /* Dynamically allocate an (m x n) matrix. Returns a pointer to the
7.   * beginning of the matrix, and NULL if allocation fails. */
8.  {
9.      double **p, *q;
10.     int i;
11.     assert(m>0 && n>0);
8
1.      /* Allocate pointer array. */
2.      p = (double **)malloc(m * sizeof(double *));
3.      if (p == NULL) return p;
12
1.      /* Allocate entire matrix as a single 1-D array. */
2.      q = (double *)malloc(m * n * sizeof (double));
3.      if (q == NULL) {
4.          free(p);
5.          return NULL;
6.      }
19
1.      /* Assign pointersinto    appropriate parts of matrix. */
2.      for (i = 0; i < m;++i, q+=n)
3.          p[i] = q;
23
1.      return p;
2.  }
```

1-11 This code is virtually identical to the previous version of create_matrix().

14-18 Rather than allocate each row separately, memory for the entire matrix is allocated as a single block. If this allocation fails, it is a simple matter to free p and return NULL. This implementation completely bypasses the goto and its more complex error-handling code.

21-22 Having allocated memory, the remaining operations cannot fail, and so do not require error checking. The pointers in the pointer array are assigned to elements in the double array at n element intervals—thus, defining the matrix.

   The destroy_matrix() code is also greatly simplified by allocating the matrix elements as a single block. First, the size of the matrix is not required, removing the possibility of passing incorrect dimension values. And, second, the deallocation operations are performed in two lines. Note, these lines must occur in the right order as p[0] is invalid if p is freed first.

```
1.  void destroy_matrix(double **p)
2.  /* Destroy a matrix. Notice, due to the method by which this matrix
3.  * was created, the size of the matrix is not required. */
4{
1.      free(p[0]);
2.      free(p);
7}
        /* Perform various matrix operations. */

        destroy_matrix(m1);
        destroy_matrix(m2);
```

## 1.    **Example: An Expandable Array**

This section presents another extended example of dynamic memory allocation, this time to demonstrate the realloc() function. realloc() is a versatile function; it can perform the tasks of both malloc() and free() and, in addition, can adjust the size of an existing dynamically allocated memory block.

In C, an array has fixed size, which is determined at compile-time. Even dynamically allocated arrays have fixed size once they have been created. In certain situations, it may be desirable to have an array that expands on demand as new elements are added to it. That is, to have an array where elements may be added to the end one-by-one, and the array grows to match the number of elements it contains; thus, the array can be built-up without knowing the number of elements in advance.

In this section, we implement an expandable array of integers. The public interface for this array is exported in a header file vector.h, which is shown below.

```
1.  /* Expandable vector, grows in-place as new elements are added to the back.
2.  * The vector memory allocation is exponential to avoid excessive copying. */
3
1.  /* Vector access operations. */
2.  int push_back(int item);
3.  int pop_back(void);
4.  int* get_element(int index);
8
9   /* Manual resizing operations. */
1.  int get_size(void);
2.  int set_size(int size);
3.  int get_capacity(void);
4.  int set_capacity(int size);
```

5-7 The vector provides three functions for element access. The first, push_back(), adds a new element to the end of the array; the second, pop_back(), returns the last element and then removes it from the array; and the third, get_element(), returns a pointer to a specified array element. The get_element() function permits the expandable vector to be accessed via pointer arithmetic like an ordinary C array.

10-13 In addition to growing the vector by adding elements to the end, there are four functions to provide control of the vector size. The first of these, get_size() and set_size(), obtain and set the size of the vector, respectively. The last two, get_capacity() and set_capacity(), directly control the reserve memory allocation for the array. These functions are explained in more detail below.

The implementation of the expandable array is defined in file vector.c. This file hides the private interface, which consists of several constants and external variables, and also hides the module's dependence on standard headers stdlib.h (for realloc()) and assert.h (for assert()).

Arrays by definition occupy a contiguous region of memory, and this creates an issue for developing an expandable array. As the array grows, it becomes necessary to request more memory, and often a region can only be extended so far before there is no more space available. At this point, if realloc() is asked to further extend the memory block, it will allocate a completely new block and *copy* the data from the old block across to the new one. An array that copies its data from one place to another every time it grows will be very inefficient, and a naive implementation will become increasingly slow. However, with an appropriate allocation scheme, an expandable array can be made to have *constant-time complexity* on average. The key is to allocate memory in geometrically increasing chunks, so that there is an ever growing amount of free-space allocated as the array size increases. This means that the frequency of allocation, and hence the cost of copying data, decreases with array size at the expense of some wasted space.

```
1. #include "vector.h"
2. #include <stdlib.h>
3. #include <assert.h>
4
```

```
1. static  const int StartSize= 1; /* initial vector size */
2. static  const float GrowthRate = 1.5;        /* geometric growth of vector  capacity */
7
```

```
1. static   int *data = NULL;/* pointer to vector elements */
2. static  int vectorsize = 0;/* current size of vector */
3. static   int capacity = 0; /* current  reserved memory for vector */
11
```

```
1.  int push_back(int item)
2.  /* Add element to back of vector. Return index of new element if successful, and -1
    if fails. */
3.  {
4.          /* If out-of-space, allocate more. */
5.          if (vectorsize == capacity) {
6.                  int newsize = (capacity == 0) ? StartSize : (int)(capacity*GrowthRate +
        1.0);
7.                  int *p = (int *)realloc(data, newsize*sizeof(int));
8.                  if (p == NULL)
9.                      return -1;
21
1.                  capacity = newsize; /* allocate succeeds, update data-structure */
2.                  data = p;
3.          }
25
1.          /* We have enough room. */
2.          data[vectorsize] = item;
3.          return vectorsize+—+;
4.  }
```

The external variables data, vectorsize, and capacity define the current state of the vector; data points to the array's dynamic memory block; vectorsize defines the current array size; and capacity records the amount of memory allocated. The value of vectorsize must always be less than or equal to capacity. Notice that these variables are all given initial values, even though they would be initialised to these values by default. Explicit initialisation improves code readability by making ones intentions clear.

1. When a new element is added to the end of the array, its size increases by one. If the vector size is already equal to the amount of available memory, additional memory must be allocated.

2. There are two cases where new memory must be allocated. One, when the very first element is pushed onto the array and, two, when an element is added that exceeds the available space. In the first case, the amount of memory requested will be some initial value StartSize and, in the second, the available memory will be increased by a multiplicative factor GrowthRate. The geometric growth value is increased by one to ensure the allocated size actually increases for small values of capacity.

18-23 The behaviour of realloc() has a few subtle points. If its first argument is NULL, then it acts like malloc() and returns a new block of memory. If the first argument is not NULL, it adjusts the passed memory block to the specified size and returns a pointer to the adjusted block. If the memory request fails, then realloc() returns NULL and the original memory block is unchanged. For this reason, the return value is assigned to a temporary pointer p, rather than

```
data = (int *)realloc(data, newsize*sizeof(int));
```

as, in the latter case, the original memory would be lost if realloc() failed. By using a temporary, push_back() can signal a failure while retaining its original state, and will only update its internal data-structures after checking that memory allocation succeeds.

27-28 Once sufficient space is known to be available, the new element is added to the array and the array size is incremented. Notice that the returned value is the value of vectorsize prior to increment, so that it represents the index of the new element.

```
1.  int pop_back(void)
2.  /* Return element from back of vector, and remove it from the vector. */
3.  {
4.      assert(vectorsize > 0);
5.      return data[ vectorsize];
6.  }
```

36

```
1.  int* get_element(int index)
2.  /* Return pointer to the element at the specified index. */
3.  {
4.      assert(index >= 0 && index < vectorsize);
5.      return data + index;
6.  }
```

30-35 The function pop_back() returns the last element of the array and then deletes it. This operation reduces the size of the array by one, but does not release any memory; capacity remains the same.

37-42 The function get_element() returns a pointer to the element specified by index. This allows the expandable array to be accessed directly and used like an ordinary array. However, pointers returned by this function should be used with caution if the array capacity subsequently changes. When realloc() allocates memory, it may copy the existing data to a new location and then release the old memory. At this instance, any pointers referring to the old memory block are invalidated and should not be dereferenced. Furthermore, if the capacity of the array is reduced, even if realloc() adjusts the memory bounds in-place, pointers referencing beyond the new bounds will be invalid.

```
1.  /* Manual size operations. */
2.  int get_size(void) { return vectorsize; }
3.  int get_capacity(void) { return capacity; }
46
1.  int set_size(int size)
2.  /* Set vector size. Return 0 if successful, -1 if fails. */
3.  {
4.       if (size>  capacity)        {
5.            int *p = (int *)realloc(data, size*sizeof(int));
6.            if (p == NULL)
7.                 return -1;
54
1.            capacity = size; /* allocate succeeds, update data-structure */
2.            data = p;
3.       }
58
1.       vectorsize =        size;
2.       return0;
3.  }
4.  int set_capacity(int size)
5.  /* Shrink or grow allocated memory reserve for array.
6.   * A size of 0 deletes the array. Return 0 if successful, -1 if fails. */
7.  {
8.       if(size !=capacity) {
9.            int *p = (int *)realloc(data, size*sizeof(int));
10.           if (p == NULL && size > 0)
11.                return -1;
71
1.            capacity = size;
2.            data = p;
3.       }
75
1.       if(size <vectorsize)
2.            vectorsize = size;
3.       return 0;
4.  }
```

44-45 These two trivial functions return the current state of the vector in terms of its size and available space, respectively.

47-61 The function set_size() changes the size of the array to the specified size. If this size is greater than the current capacity, then extra memory is allocated to suit. However, if the size is reduced, capacity is left unchanged; this function cannot decrease the available storage.

63-79 The function set_capacity() provides direct access to the memory allocation of the vector. It can be used to increase or decrease the available storage. If the requested size is less than the current vector size, the vector is truncated to fit. If the requested size is zero, realloc() will release the memory pointed to by its first argument and return NULL, effectively deleting the vector. Notice that a request of size zero, will cause data to become NULL (line 73), and vectorsize and capacity to become zero—thus, returning the vector to its original state.

The above implementation of an expandable array is a good example of modular programming as far as it goes, but it is subject to a couple of serious limitations. First, it provides a single instance of the vector only, and we cannot have more than one in any given program. Second, the vector can only contain elements of type int. To create a vector for other types would require a new, virtually identical, implementation for each type. Neither of these limitations are insurmountable, but they require the use of language features not yet covered, such as structs, unions, typedef, and the void* pointer. The application of these features to writing generic code, is the subject of Chapter 14.

# Chapter 10

## The C Preprocessor

*The C preprocessor is a simple macro processor that conceptually processes the source text of a C program before the compiler proper reads the source program...*

*The preprocessor is controlled by special preprocessor command lines, which are lines of the source file beginning with the character #. Lines that do not contain preprocessor commands are called lines of the program text...*

*The preprocessor removes all preprocessor command lines from the source file and makes additional transformations on the source file as directed by the commands, such as expanding macro calls that occur within the source program text. The resulting preprocessed source text must then be a valid C program.*

*The syntax of preprocessor commands is completely independent of (though in some ways similar to) the syntax of the rest of the C language [HS95, page 39].*

The C preprocessor performs a variety of text replacement operations on the source text before it is parsed by the C compiler. These operations include replacing symbolic names with constants, expansion of macros, and inclusion of header-files. A preprocessor directive, such as #define, has file scope, meaning that defined names are visible from their point of declaration until the end of the source file in which they appear.

The operations of the preprocessor are not subject to the syntactical rules of the C language, and so should be used sparingly and with care. In particular, the text substitution of macro expansion changes the lexical structure of the source code and may produce unexpected behaviour if certain pitfalls are not avoided.

1.      **File Inclusion**

One of the most common uses of the preprocessor is for the inclusion of files into the source text. These are usually header files, but may be any text file. The file include command is

  #include

and it is followed by a file name enclosed in either <> or "". The result of this command after preprocessing is as if the command were replaced by the text of the specified file. Further details with regard to the #include directive are discussed in Section 5.6.

1.      **Symbolic Constants**

2.      The preprocessor may be used to define symbolic constants via the #define command. The general form of a symbolic constant definition is as follows

replacement text

#define name

  whereby name becomes a placeholder for the character sequence replacement text. Given this command, the preprocessor will replace all subsequent occurrences of the token name in the source file by the sequence replacement text. Some example symbolic constants are

    #define
    BUFFERSIZE
    256        #define
    MIN_VALUE   -
    32 #define PI        3.14159

A name created by #define can be undefined using the directive #undef. This name may then be used to represent a different sequence of replacement text.

Style Note. Symbolic constants are usually given uppercase names to differentiate them from variable and function names. The #define command is also used to define macros, and these names are also usually uppercase.

  C provides several different mechanisms for defining names for numerical constants. The preprocessor directive #define can create names for constants of any type; the type qualifier const can define constant variables of any type; and the keyword enum can define constants of integer type. Each of these is better suited to certain situations than the others. The #define command is most powerful, and can be used in any situation where the other two might be used, but it is also the most dangerous as the preprocessor does not respect C syntax rules. Variables qualified by const are generally preferred but, as these variables are not considered *compile-time* constant, they have one significant limitation; namely, a variable of type const int cannot be used to define the size of an array.

```
#define ARRAYSIZE  10
const int ArraySize = 10; double
array1[ARRAYSIZE]; /* Valid. */
double array2[ArraySize]; /* Invalid.
*/
```

An enumeration constant does not suffer this limitation and, between them, const and enum can satisfy all symbolic constant operations for which a #define might be used. As const and enum are part of the C language proper, and abide by its rules, they are to be preferred over #define in general. For example,

```
#define PI              3.14159
#define ARRAYSIZE10
const double Pi = 3.14159; /*
Preferred */ enum { ARRAYSIZE=10
};                              /*
Preferred */
```

1.      **Macros**

Symbolic constants defined by the #define command are a simple form of macro: a symbolic name that is expanded into an expression via text substitution. The C preprocessor provides a more sophisticated type of macro definition by allowing the macro name to be followed by a set of arguments enclosed in parentheses. For example,

```
#define MAX(x,y) ((x)>(y) ? (x) : (y))
```

Although it looks like a function call, a macro behaves in a quite different manner. The preprocessor replaces the macro name with the defined replacement text, and substitutes the argument variables in the specified locations. Thus, MAX might be used as follows

```
int a=4, b=
-7, c; c =
MAX(a,b);
```

and the preprocessor will expand the code to

```
int a=4, b= -7, c; c =
((a)>(b) ? (a) : (b));
```

Note. In a macro definition, the parentheses immediately following the macro name must be directly adjacent to the name without whitespace. For example, the definition

```
#define MAX (x,y)   ((x)>(y) ? (x) : (y))
```

is not equivalent to the previous macro definition, but will simply replace all occurrences of the name MAX with the text: (x,y)   ((x)>(y) ? (x) : (y)).

Macros are typically used for one of two reasons. The first is speed. Macros can perform functionlike operations without the overhead of a function call because the code is expanded inline. With modern fast machines, using macros for speed is less important than it used to be. The second use of macros is to implement a kind of *generic function.* That is, to define a function-like expression that bypasses the C type constraints, and can be passed parameters of any type. For example, the macro MAX will work correctly if a, b, and c were type double, or any other type, where as an equivalent function

```
int max(int x, int y)
{
    return x > y ? x : y;
}
```

will only accept integer parameters.

1.      **Macro Basics**

Consider the following simple macros.

```
#define SQR(x)
#define SGN(x)
#define ABS(x)
#define ISDIGIT(x) #define NELEMS(array)
((x)*(x))
(((x)<0) ? -1 : 1)
(((x)<0) ? -(x) : (x))
((x) >= '0' && (x) <= '9') (sizeof(array) / sizeof(array[0]))
```

SQR calculates the square of its argument, SGN calculates the sign of its argument, ABS converts its argument to an absolute value, ISDIGIT equals 1 if the argument value is between the character code for 0 and the character code for 9, and NELEMS computes the number of elements in an array.

Macros should be used with care. The preprocessor is a powerful but rather blunt instrument, and it is easy to use macros incorrectly. Macros are subject to three main dangers. The first is that the passed arguments may have surprising precedence after macro expansion. For example, if SQR were defined as

```
#define SQR(x)        x * x
```

then the following expression

```
int a = 7; b = SQR(a+1);
```

will expand to

```
b = a+1 * a+1; /* b equals 7 + 1*7 + 1 = 15, not the expected 64 */
```

For this reason, macro arguments should be heavily parenthesised as with the set of examples above.

The second danger is that arguments with side-effects may be evaluated multiple times after macro expansion. For example,

```
b = ABS(a++);
```

will expand to

```
b = (((a++)<0) ? -(a++) : (a++));
```

so that a is incremented twice, which is not the expected behaviour. To avoid these sort of problems, it is good practice to never use expressions with side-effects as macro arguments. The final danger is that the ability to bypass the C type-checking system is a double-edged sword. It permits greater flexibility, but also prevents the compiler from catching some type-mismatch bugs.

In general, functions are to be preferred over macros as they are safer. However, with a little care, macros can be used without significant trouble, when required.

1.      **More Macros**

There are many neat and ingenious macros to be found in existing source code, and there is much to be learned from other peoples invention. The following two examples are simple and clever.

```
#define CLAMP(val,low,high) ((val)<(low) ? (low) : (val) > (high) ? (high) : (val))
#define ROUND(val)          ((val)>0 ? (int)((val)+0.5) : -(int)(0.5-(val)))
```

The first, CLAMP, uses two nested ?: expressions to bound a value val so that if it is less-than low it becomes equal to low, and if it is greater-than high it becomes equal to high, otherwise it remains unchanged. The second macro, ROUND, rounds a floating-point value to the nearest integer. It performs this operation using the truncation properties of casting a double to an int, but contains one clever subtlety. The truncation by casting to int is straightforward if the value is positive, but machine dependent if the value is negative (see Section 2.7). ROUND gets around this problem by subtracting the negative value from 0.5, thus making a positive value, and then negating the answer.

Another clever macro trick is used to make macros behave more like functions. Consider the following macro that swaps two variables (using an additional temporary value).

```
#define SWAP(x,y,tmp) { tmp=x; x=y; y=tmp; }
```

This operation might be used as in the next example

```
int a=4, b=-1, temp;
SWAP(a, b, temp);
```

However, this macro will not behave in a function-like manner if used in an if-statement

```
if (a > b) SWAP(a, b, temp); /* Won't compile */ else a = b;
```

as this code will be expanded to incorrect C syntax.

```
if (a > b) { temp=a; a=b; b=temp; }
;
else a = b;
```

A solution to this problem is to wrap the body of the macro in a do-while statement, which will consume the offending semicolon.

```
#define SWAP(x,y,tmp) do { tmp=x; x=y; y=tmp; } while (0)
```

An alternative solution is to wrap the macro in an if-else statement.

```
#define SWAP(x,y,tmp) if(1) { tmp=x; x=y; y=tmp; } else
```

A variant of SWAP does away with defining an explicit temporary variable by simply passing the variable type to the macro.

```
#define SWAP(x,y,type) do { type tmp=x; x=y; y=tmp; } while (0)
```

This might be used as

SWAP(a, b, double);

Finally, a very tricky *bitwise* technique allows us to perform the swap operation without any temporary variable at all. (However, this variant is only valid if x and y are integer variables of the same type.)

```
#define SWAP(x,y)        do { x"=y; y"=x; x"=y; } while (0)
```

## 1.    More Complex Macros

Normally a macro definition extends to the end of the line beginning with the command #define. However, long macros can be split over several lines by placing a \ at the end of the line to be continued. For example,

```
#define ERROR(condition,
       message) \ if (condition)
       printf(message)
```

A more interesting example, adapted from [KP99, page 240], performs a timing loop on a section of code using the standard library function clock(), which returns processor time in milliseconds.

```
#define TIMELOOP(CODE) {         \
       t0 = clock();              \
       for (i = 0; i<n; ++i) { CODE;
       } \ printf("%7d ", clock() - t0);    \
}
```

This macro might be used as follows.

```
TIMELOOP(y = sin(x));
```

It is possible to convert a token to a string constant by writing a macro that uses the # symbol in the manner of the following example.

```
#define PRINT_DEBUG(expr) printf(#expr " = %g\n", expr)
```

This macro when invoked will print the expression and its result, as the first instance of the expression is converted to a string constant by the preceding #. For example,

```
PRINT_DEBUG(x/y);
```

is expanded to

```
printf("x/y" " = °/.g\n", x/y);
```

Another rather obscure preprocessor operator is ##, which provides a way to concatenate two tokens. For example,

```
#define TEMP(i) temp ## i
```

might be used to create different temporary

variable names TEMP(1) = TEMP(2); which,

after preprocessing, becomes

```
temp1 = temp2;
```

The preprocessor defines a number of predefined macros. These are LINE , FILE , _DATE , TIME , STDC , and STDC_VERSION . Notice that each of these names is prefixed and suffixed by double underscore characters. Determining the meaning of each of these macros is left as an exercise to the reader.

To put the various aspects of this section together, consider the following macro,

```
#define PRINT_DEBUG(expr, type) \
          printf("File: " __FILE__ \
"\nLine: %d\nExpr: " #expr \
" = %" type##TYPE "\n", __LINE__, (expr))
```

which, given a set of definitions for formatting different types, e.g.,

```
#define intTYPE        "d"

#define doubleTYPE     "f"
```

can be used as

```
    PRINT_DEBUG(x/y, double);
```

which will print the source-file name, the statement line number, the expression and its value. Indeed a clever and useful debugging macro.

# 1.      **Conditional Compilation**

The C preprocessor provides a series of directives for conditional compilation: #if, #elif, #else, #ifdef, #ifndef, and #endif. These commands cause the preprocessor to include or exclude sections of the source code from compilation depending on certain conditions. Conditional compilation is used for three main purposes: to optionally include debug code, to enclose non-portable code, and to guard against multiple inclusion of header files.

It is common to write short sections of code exclusively for debugging purposes; this is often called "instrumentation". This code should be present in the program during a debug build but removed for the final release build. However, it is a good idea to not actually delete the code, but to optionally include it using a preprocessor condition so that it is still available if further debugging is required. Typically, during debug builds, one defines a symbolic constant DEBUG so that debug code is included. For example,

```
#ifdef DEBUG
      printf(MPointer %#x points to value %f", pd, *pd);
#endif
```

When writing a program that contains non-portable code, it is good practice to isolate the nonportable parts in a separate source file. The different code sections for different machines are then enclosed in preprocessor conditions so that only the code for the specified machine is compiled. For example,

```
#ifdef __WIN32 /* Code specific to Windows. */
      return WaitForSingleObject(handle, 0) == WAIT_OBJECT_0;

#elif defined(__QNX) || defined(__linux__) /* Code specific to QNX or Linux. */
      if(flock(fd, LOCK_EX | LOCK_NB) == -1) return 0;
      else return 1;
#endif
```

A header file should only be included once in any given source file (although they may appear in any number of *different* source files in the program). Otherwise certain symbols might obtain multiple definitions, which would result in a compilation error.

This problem can occur if some header files include other header files, such that several headers are dependent on a common header file. To prevent the problem of multiple inclusion, the following preprocessor idiom is applied. Consider a header file aheader.h, which begins and ends with the preprocessor commands below.

```
#ifndef A_HEADER_H_

#define A_HEADER_H_

/* Contents of header file is contained here. */

#endif
```

By prefixing the file with #ifndef A_HEADER_H_, the header is included the first time (presuming A_HEADER_H_ is not defined previously), but A_HEADER_H_ is subsequently defined in the next line. This prevents any subsequent inclusion of the header for a given source-file. This idiom is known as a "header guard".

# Chapter 11

## Structures and Unions

*A structure is a collection of one or more variables, possibly of different types, grouped together under a single name for convenient handling. ... Structures help to organise complicated data, particularly in large programs, because they permit a group of related variables to be treated as a unit instead of as separate entities [KR88, page 127].*

The C language provides means to create user-defined types called *structures*. These types are aggregates of basic types and other user-defined types, and permit a logical grouping of related data. This chapter discusses structures, their operations and implications, and the associated topics of type-definitions and unions.

## 1.      Structures

A structure is declared using the keyword struct, and the internal organisation of the structure is defined by a set of variables enclosed in braces. Consider the following example, which declares a structure for representing two-dimensional points.

```
struct Point { int x; int y;
};
```

Style Note. By convention, structures should always be named with an uppercase first letter. This distinguishes them from variables and functions (lowercase first letter), and symbolic constants (all uppercase).

The variables x and y are called *members* of the structure named Point. Variables of type Point may be defined as a list of identifiers at the end of the struct definition,

```
struct Point { int x; int y;
} p1, p2, p3; /* Define three variables of type Point. */
```

or as subsequent definitions using the tag "struct Point".

```
struct Point p1, p2, p3; /* Define three variables of type Point. */
```

When a structure is defined, its members may be initialised using brace notation as follows.

```
struct Point topleft = { 320, 0 };
```

Here the member x is initialised to 320 and the member y to 0. In general, the values within the initialiser list correspond to the structure member variables in order of their declaration.

Individual members of a struct may be accessed via the *member operator* ". ". For example,

```
struct Point topleft; topleft.x = 320; topleft.y = 0;
```

is an alternative way to initialise the variable topleft. Thus, we might compute the distance between two points pt1 and pt2, using the standard library function sqrt(), as shown below.

```
struct Point delta = { pt1.x - pt2.x, pt1.y - pt2.y };
double distance = sqrt((double)delta.x * delta.x + (double)delta.y * delta.y);
```

Structures can be nested, such that the definition of one structure type may be composed, in part, of another structure type. For example, a rectangle might be described by its top-left and bottom-right corners as follows.

```
struct Rectangle {
    struct Point topleft; struct
    Point bottomright;
};
```

To access the lowest-level members of a variable of type Rectangle, therefore, requires two instances of the member operator.

```
struct Rectangle rect; rect.topleft.x = 50;
```

1.     **Operations on Structures**

The operations permitted on structures are a subset of the operations permitted on basic types (such as int, double, etc). Structures may be copied or assigned, but it is not possible to directly compare two structures.

```
struct Point p1 = { 0, 0 }; struct Point p2;

p2 = p1;          /* Valid. structs may be assigned. */
if (p1 == p2)     /* Invalid. structs may not be compared. */
    printf("Points are equal\n");
if (p1.x == p2.x && p1.y == p2.y) /* Valid. May compare basic types. */
    printf("Points are equal\n");
```

A structure may be passed to a function and may be returned by a function.

```
struct Point point_difference(struct Point p1, struct Point p2)
/* Return the delta (dx, dy) of p2 with respect to p1. */
{
    p2.x -= p1.x;
    p2.y -= p1.y;
    return p2;
}
```

As with any other variable, structures are passed by value. Thus, in the above example, pi and p2 are *copies* of the passed arguments, and the changes to p2 within the function do not affect the value of the associated variable in the calling function.

```
struct Point a = {5,10}, b = {20,30}, c;
c = point_difference(a, b); /* c = {15,20}, b is unchanged. */
```

Passing structures by value can be inefficient if the structure is large, and it is generally more efficient to pass a pointer to a struct rather than making a copy. Defining structure pointers and obtaining the address of a struct variable is the same as for basic types.

```
struct Point pt = { 50, 50 }; struct Point *pp;

pp = &pt;
(*pp).x = 100; /* pt.x is now 100. */
```

Note, the parentheses about (*pp).x are necessary to enforce the correct order-of-evaluation, so that the pointer-to-struct is dereferenced *before* attempting to access member x. To avoid this rather complicated dereferencing syntax, an alternative notation is provided to access structure members via a pointer. The -> operator permits the expression (*pp).x to be rewritten more simply as
pp->x.

As a further example, given the variable definitions

```
struct Rectangle rect, *pr = &rect;
```

the following statements are equivalent.

```
rect.topleft.x = 50;
(*pr).topleft.x = 50; pr->topleft.x = 50;
```

1.      **Arrays of Structures**

As for basic types, it is possible to create an array of structures.

```
struct Point pa[10];
```

The elements of the array may be initialised by a brace-enclosed initialiser list and, when doing so, the size of the array need not be specified. The example below defines an array of four elements.

```
struct Point pa[] = {
    {0, 0}, {0, 240}, {320, 240}, {320, 0}
};
```

The size of a structure type in bytes may be computed using the sizeof operator, and the number of elements in the above array can be found using the idiom

```
int nelems = sizeof(pa) / sizeof(pa[0]);
```

As for basic types, pointer arithmetic for structure types is managed by the compiler, so that the operations

```
struct Point *pp = pa;
for (; pp != pa + sizeof(pa) / sizeof(pa[0]); ++pp) printf("%d
    %d\n", pp->x, pp->y);
```

will effectively print the (x,y) values of each element in the array. The compiler knows the size of the structure type and determines the appropriate address offsets accordingly.

Important. The size of a structure might not equal the sum of its constituent parts. For example, if we assume a char is one byte and an int is four bytes, the following structure type

```
struct Stype {
    char c;
    int i;
};
```

might not have size five bytes. Most real machines require objects to satisfy certain alignment restrictions (e.g., integers must be located at even addresses), and the compiler will pad the structure with unnamed "holes" to ensure each member is properly aligned. Thus, the above example might have size six or eight bytes rather than five bytes. The sizeof operator returns the correct value.

1.   **Self-Referential Structures**

A structure definition may not contain an object of its own type,

```
struct Node {
    int item;
    struct Node next; /* Invalid. Cannot define an object of an incomplete type. */
}
```

but it may refer to a *pointer* of its own type.

```
struct Node {
    int item;
    struct Node *next; /* Valid. May define a pointer to an incomplete type. */
}
```

The ability of a structure to refer to incomplete types (including itself) via a pointer is a vital property for constructing a number of important data-structures. These include linked-lists, binary trees, graphs, hash tables, and many more.

The following example demonstrates a simple linked-list implementation. Linked-lists come in two main varieties: singly-linked and doubly-linked. The former consists of a series of nodes containing a value and a pointer to another node. Each node is defined as follows.

```
struct
    List
    { int
    item;
    struct List *next;
};
```

Figure 11.1: Singly linked-list. Each node in the list contains an item and a pointer to the next node in the list. A pointer to the first node is called the head. The end node points to NULL to signify the end of the list.
In this example, the value contained by the node is an integer variable, but it could be a variable of any type. The set of nodes are connected such that the next pointer for each node points to the address of the next node in the list as shown in Figure 11.1. The end of the list is marked by a node whose next pointer is NULL.

To traverse a singly linked-list, it is necessary to hold a pointer to the first node in the list; this pointer refers to the head of the list. The subsequent nodes may be accessed by iterating through each node in turn. For example, the code segment below shows how to reach the end node.

```
struct List *node = head;
while (node->next != NULL)
    node = node->next;
```

Linked-lists are useful for their ability to be grown and shrunk easily without issues of memory reallocation and data copying. It is straightforward to add and delete elements, even to splice elements into the middle to the list. The function below demonstrates a list-growing implementation that adds a new node to the end of the list. The first argument may be a pointer to the head of the list, or a pointer to any node midway along the list, and the function will find the end and attach a new node to it. If the function is passed NULL, it creates a new head node and returns a pointer to it.

```
struct List *insert_back(struct List *node, int item)
/* Add new item to the end of the list. Return pointer to the new List node. */
{
    /* Allocate memory for new node. */
    struct List *newnode = (struct List *)
    malloc(sizeof(struct List)); if (newnode ==
    NULL)
        return NULL; /* allocation failed */

    newnode—>item = item; newnode—>next =
    NULL;

    /* If list is not empty, find end of list and attach
    new node. */ if (node) {
        while (node—>next)
            node =
        node—>next;
        node—>next =
        newnode;
    }

    return newnode;
```

**head**

Figure 11.2: Inserting a new node into the middle of a singly linked-list. Prior to insertion, the next pointer of node A points to node B. A new node, C, is created, and its next pointer is made to point to B and the next pointer of node A is made to point to C.

The following function inserts a node at a specified location in the list. A pointer to the node *one before* the insertion is passed to the function, and its next pointer is used to splice the new node into the next position in the list, as shown in Figure 11.2.

```
/* Allocate memory for new node. */
struct List *newnode = (struct List *)
malloc(sizeof(struct List)); if (newnode == NULL)
        return NULL; /* allocation failed */

/* If list is not empty, splice new node into list. */ if
(node) {
        newnode—> next = node-
        >next; node—>next =
        newnode;
}
else newnode—> next = NULL;

newnode—>item = item; return newnode;
```

A doubly linked-list is similar to a singly linked-list except that each node also contains a pointer to the previous node in the list as follows.

```
struct List {
    int item;
    struct List *next;
    struct List *prev;
};
```

NULL

Figure 11.3: Doubly linked-list. Each node contains a pointer to the next and the previous node in the list. The ends of the list in both directions are marked by NULL pointers.

The enables the list to be constructed as shown in Figure 11.3, and permits traversal up the list as well as down. In particular, doubly linked-lists make the deletion of elements simpler and more efficient than is possible with a singly linked-list.

*1.*     **Typedefs**

> *In effect* typedef *is like* #define, *except that since it is interpreted by the compiler, it can cope with textual substitutions beyond the capabilities of the preprocessor [KR88, page 147].*

The keyword typedef provides a means for creating new data type names. It does not create a new type, but merely adds a new name for some existing type. For example,

```
typedef int Length;
```

makes the name Length a synonym for int. The type Length may then be used wherever the type int might be used.

```
Length len, maxlen;
Length lengths[50];
```

In relation to structures, the ability to define type synonyms permits a significant improvement in structure declaration syntax. For example, the following declaration

```
typedef struct Point {
      int x; int y;
} Point;
```

permits subsequent definitions of type Point to be written as

```
Point ptl, pt2;
```

without the preceding struct keyword. This simplification is more marked for self-referencing structures, such as for a linked-list.

```
typedef struct list_t List;
struct list_t { int item;
      List *next;
};
```

Link-list nodes are subsequently defined as type List. Notice that the typedefed name need not match the original structure tag; and for non-self-referencing structures, such as Point above, the structure-tag may be neglected altogether.

There are four main reasons for using typedef. The first is to improve the appearance of declaration syntax as shown above. This is perhaps best exemplified by the ability of typedef to break up complicated declarations such as arrays-of-pointers-to-functions (as shown in Section 8.4). The second reason for using typedef is that type-synonyms often provide better in-code documentation than a plain type. For example, the type Length gives a better indication of a variable's purpose than just an int, and makes the code more readable. The third use of typedef is to shield a program from portability problems.

> *If* typedef *s are used for data types that may be machine dependent, only the* typedef *s need change when the program is moved. One common situation is to use* typedef *names for various integer quantities, then make an appropriate set of choices of* short, int, *and* long *for each host machine. Types like* size_t *and* ptrdiff_t *from the standard library are examples. [KR88, page 147]*

The typedef names localise the definition of non-portable types to a single location, rather than having them sprinkled throughout the code. For example, on a 32-bit machine, two-byte and four- byte integer types may be defined as follows,

```
typedef short INT16;
typedef int INT32;
```

while, on a 16-bit machine, the same size integers are defined as

```
typedef int INT16; typedef
long INT32;
```

The fourth reason for using typedef is to facilitate a basic form of generic programming. In the linked-list examples above, each node contains an item of type int. By defining the contained type with a typedef, the list can be made to contain objects of different types.

```
typedef int ValueType;
typedef struct List {
    ValueType item;
    struct List *next;
} List;
```
The algorithms that use the link-list must also use the typedefed name.

```
List *insert_back(List *node, ValueType item);
List *insert_after(List *node, ValueType item);
```

With these alterations, the code can be made to operate on a different type with the change of a single line of code.


1.       **Object-Oriented Programming Style**

Functions and structures work together to facilitate a basic style of object-oriented programming in terms of encapsulation and modularity. The synergy of these features permits a more modular coding style than is possible with either feature in isolation.

Encapsulation refers to the ability to hide the implementation details of a code module so that only a high-level abstraction of the code is visible to the client. The client knows *what* a module does but does not need to know how it does it. Functions facilitate modularity by hiding algorithm details behind a well-defined interface. Structures perform a similar task by hiding data representation details within a higher-level type definition. Used in combination, it is possible to define abstract data types and manipulate them via functions, thus hiding implementation details and presenting only a conceptual view to the client via the public interface.

This design principle is evident in the previous linked-list example, where the client need only be aware of a List type object, and various functions for adding elements to the list. The client does not need to know anything about the actual representation of the linked-list, or the algorithms for adding the elements.

The following is another simple example of object-oriented program design. Consider a structure that represents a complex number type.

```
typedef struct {
    double real;
    double
    imag;
} Complex;
```

The set of functions shown below perform a variety of operations on these complex number variables. They perform object creation, addition and multiplication of two complex numbers, in-place addition and multiplication, and comparison of two complex numbers. In each case, the client does not need to know how the functions perform their tasks, but simply what type of result is expected when they return.

```
Complex make_complex(double r, double i)
/* Construct a Complex object with the initial values r and i. */
{
    Comple
    x c;
    c.real =
    r;
    c.imag
    = i;
    return c;
```

```
}
Complex add_complex(Complex a, Complex b)
/* Add two complex numbers and return the result. */
{
        Complex sum; sum.real = a.real +
        b.real; sum.imag = a.imag + b.imag;
        return sum;
}

Complex mult_complex(Complex a, Complex b)
/* Multiply two complex numbers and return the result. */
{
        Complex prod;
        prod.real = a.real*b.real —
        a.imag*b.imag; prod.imag =
        a.real*b.imag + a.imag*b.real; return
        prod;
}
void addequal_complex(Complex* a, const Complex* b)
/* Add two complex numbers and store the result in a. */
{
        a—>real += b—>real; a—>imag +=
        b—>imag;
}
void multequal_complex(Complex* a, const Complex* b)
/* Multiply two complex numbers and store the
result in a. */{
        a—>real = a—>real*b—>real — a—
        >imag*b—>imag; a—>imag = a—
        >real*b—>imag + a—>imag*b—>real;
}

int is_equal(Complex a, Complex b)
/* Return TRUE if the values of a and b are equal. */
{
        return a.real == b.real && a.imag == b.imag;
}
```

1.      **Expandable Array Revisited**

In Section 9.5, we examined an expandable array that grows on demand as new elements
are added to it. The code presented was modular and flexible, but has two major
limitations. First, it permits a program to have only one vector object and, second, the
vector may only contain items of type int. Using structures and typedef, we can overcome
these two problems, allowing us to create any number of vectors, and use the same code
to produce vectors of different types.
    The header file vector.h for the expandable vector is shown below. It is similar to the
original code, but includes a typedef ValueType for the contained type and a struct
Vector defining the format of the vector type. By simply changing line 4 to

    typedef char ValueType;

the vector can be made to contain elements of type char, and similarly for other types.

The structure Vector groups together the three essential variables to represent a vector object: its size, capacity, and a pointer to the allocated array itself.

It is important to realise that because Vector objects are manipulated exclusively by the associated functions declared in lines 13 to 25, the user does not actually need to know how the Vector type is composed. All that the client needs to understand is what task each function in the public interface performs. Access to the Vector internals is managed by functions like get_element() and get_size(), etc. Because of this decoupling, the internal make up of struct Vector may be changed and, similarly, the function algorithms may be changed, all without affecting client code.

```
/* Vector: an expandable vector type that contains elements of type ValueType.
*/
typedef double

ValueType; typedef

struct {
        ValueType *data; /* pointer to vector elements */
        int size;        /* current size of vector */
        int capacity; /* current reserved memory for vector */
} Vector;

/* Vector creation and destruction. */
Vector create_vector(int
capacity); void
release_vector(Vector
*v);

/* Vector access operations. */
int push_back(Vector *v, ValueType item);
ValueType pop_back(Vector *v);
ValueType* get_element(Vector *v, int index);

/* Manual resizing operations. */
int get_size(Vector *v);
int set_size(Vector *v, int size);
int get_capacity(Vector *v);
int set_capacity(Vector *v, int size);
```

The operations performed by the public interface are essentially the same as for the original vector implementation. Two new functions

```
Vector create_vector(int capacity);
void release_vector(Vector *v);
```

are used to initialise the internal data of a vector object and to release the data of a vector object, respectively. Having created a vector object, it may be passed to the other functions (via a pointer) to perform various operations.

The implementation of the expandable vector involves only minor modifications from the original implementation. All references to int-type elements have been changed to ValueType, and operations are carried out using a pointer to a vector object. The code of source file vector.c is shown below.

```
#include "vector.h"
#include <stdlib.h>
#include <assert.h>
```

```c
static const int StartSize = 5; /* initial vector capacity */
static const float GrowthRate = 1.6f; /* geometric growth of vector capacity */

Vector create_vector(int capacity)
/* Initialise a vector with the specified capacity. */
{
    Vector
    v;
    v.size =
    0;
    v.data = (ValueType
    *)malloc(capacity*sizeof(ValueType));
    v.capacity = (v.data == NULL) ? 0 : capacity;
    return v;
}

void release_vector(Vector *v)
/* Release memory owned by vector. */
{
    free(v->data); v—
    >size = 0; v—
    >capacity = 0;
}

int push_back(Vector *v, ValueType item)
/* Add element to back of vector. Return index of new element if successful, and -1 if
fails. */
{
    /* If out-of-space, allocate
    more. */ if (v—>size == v—
    >capacity) {
        int newsize = (v—>capacity == 0) ? StartSize : (int)(v—
        >capacity*GrowthRate + 1.0); ValueType *p = (ValueType
        *)realloc(v—>data, newsize*sizeof(ValueType)); if (p == NULL)
            return —1;

        v—>capacity = newsize; /* allocate succeeds, update data-structure */
        v—>data = p;
    }

    /* We have enough room. */ v—
    >data[v—>size] = item; return
    v—>size+—+;
}

ValueType pop_back(Vector *v)
/* Return element from back of vector, and remove it from the vector. */
{
    assert(v—>size > 0); return v—
    >data[——v—>size];
}

ValueType* get_element(Vector *v, int index)
/* Return pointer to the element at the specified index. */
{
    assert(index >= 0 && index <
    v—>size); return v—>data +
    index;
```

```
} /* Manual size operations. */
int get_size(Vector *v) { return v—>size; }
int get_capacity(Vector *v) { return v—>capacity; }

int set_size(Vector *v, int size)
/* Set vector size. Return 0 if successful, -1 if fails. */
{
        if (size > v—>capacity) {
                ValueType *p = (ValueType *)realloc(v—>data,
                size*sizeof(ValueType)); if (p == NULL)
                        return —1;

                v—>capacity = size; /* allocate succeeds, update data-structure */ v—
                >data = p;
        }
        v—>size = size;
        return 0;
}

int set_capacity(Vector *v, int size)
/* Shrink or grow allocated memory reserve for array.
* A size of 0 deletes the array. Return 0 if successful, -1 if fails. */
{
        if (size != v—>capacity) {
                ValueType *p = (ValueType *)realloc(v—>data, size*sizeof(ValueType));
                if (p == NULL && size > 0)
                        return -1;

                v—>capacity = size;
                v—>data = p;
        }

        if (size < v—>size)
                v—>size = size;
        return 0;
}
```

The result of this code is an expandable vector library that can create and operate on any number of vector objects. These vectors can contain elements of type ValueType which is specified at compile time.

The code has an object-oriented style, where a high-level data type is defined using a structure (Vector), and operations on the structure are performed exclusively by a set of associated functions. The client is shielded from the data representation and algorithmic details; these aspects may be changed without affecting client code. The synergy of structures, functions and file-modularity permits highly modular and flexible code design.

This code still has one limitation remaining. Vectors can be made to contain elements of different types, but not at the same time. In a given program, all vectors must contain the same type. This limitation can be overcome using the facility of the generic object pointer void*. We return to the topic of generic programming in Chapter 14.


*1.*     **Unions**

*A union is a variable that may hold (at different times) objects of different types and sizes, with the compiler keeping track of size and alignment requirements. Unions provide a way to manipulate different kinds of data in a single area of storage, without embedding any machine-dependent information in the program [KR88, page 147].*

The declaration of a union type is similar to the declaration of a struct type. For example,

```
union Utype { int ival; float fval; char *sval;
};

union Utype x, y, z; /* Define variables of type Utype. */
```

Accessing members of a union type is also the same as for structures, with the . member operator for union objects and the -> operator for pointers to union objects.

However, the behaviour of union variables is quite different to structures. Where a struct defines a group of related variables and provides storage for all of its members, a union provides storage for a *single* variable, which may be one of several types. In the above example, the compiler will allocate sufficient memory to store the largest of the types int, float, and char *. At any given time, a Utype variable holds a value for one of the three possible types, and it is the programmers responsibility to keep track of which type that might be. The type retrieved must be the same as the type most recently stored, and the result of retrieving a different type is implementation dependent.

```
union Utype x;
x.fval =56.4;              /* x holds type float. */
printf("%f\n", x.fval); /* OK. */
printf("%d\n", x.ival); /* Implementation dependent. */
```

Unions are usually used for one of three purposes. The first is to create a "variant" array—an array that can hold heterogeneous elements. This can be performed with a reasonable degree of type safety by wrapping the union within a structure which records the union variable's current type. For example,

```
typedef union { /* Heterogeneous type. */ int ival; float fval;

} Utype;

enum { INT, FLOAT }; /* Define type tags. */ typedef struct {
        int type; /* Tag for the current stored type. */
        Utype val; /* Storage for variant type. */
} VariantType;

VariantType array[50]; /* Heterogeneous array. */ array[0].val.ival = 56; /*
Assign value. */ array[0].type = INT; /* Mark type. */


for (i = 0; i < sizeof(array)/sizeof(array[0]); ++i) /* Print array. */ if
    (array[i].type == INT)
        printf("%d\n", array[i].val.ival);
    else if (array[i].type == FLOAT)
        printf("/f\n", array[i].val.fval);
    else
        printf("Unknown type\n");
```

Checking for the correct type remains the programmer's responsibility, but encoding the variable type in a structure eases the pain of recording the current state.

The second use of a union is to enforce the alignment of a variable to a particular address boundary. This is a valuable property for implementing memory allocation functions. And the third key use of a union is to get "under the hood" of C's type system to discover something about the computer's underlying data representation. For example, to print the representation of a floating-point number, one might use the following function (assuming int and float are both four-bytes).

```
void print_representation(float f)
/* Print internal representation of a float (adapted from H&S page 145). */
{
    union { float f; int i; } fi = f;
    printf("The representation of /e is /#x\n", fi.f, fi.i);
}
```

Both the second and third uses of unions described here are advanced topics, and a more complete discussion is beyond the scope of this text.

# Chapter 12

## Bitwise Operations

C provides operators for direct manipulation of bits and bytes. These operators, and other facilities such as pointers and casts, enable C to perform low-level operations that are typically the domain of assembly languages. With care, many of these low-level functions can be implemented in a portable fashion. However, for some programs (e.g., embedded systems), it may be necessary to write nonportable specific code to interface with particular hardware devices. In these cases, it is critical to be able to control the individual bits corresponding to the device pins.

1.    **Binary Representations**

Computers store and manipulate information as bits—ones and zeros. These are grouped in cells or *bytes,* usually composed of eight bits, and each byte of memory is located by a particular address. In C, the various types each specify a certain number of bytes, and variables of a particular type are allocated the required amount of memory. The numerical value of a variable is stored as a bit-pattern within its allocated memory region.
    Consider a 16-bit (two-byte) integer with the decimal value 22425. This value is stored as the following bit pattern.

    0101 0111 1001 1001

Since the number is in base 2, each digit from right-to-left represents a successive power of two ($2^0, 2^1, .. 2^{15}$). The right-most bit is called the *least-significant bit* (LSB) and the left-most bit is the *most-significant bit* (MSB). For signed types, a value is negative if the MSB is 1, and the MSB is termed the *sign bit.* Most machines store negative values in 2's-complement form, such that the value -22425 is represented as

    1010 1000 0110 0111

The conversion of a negative number to 2's-complement form is straightforward. For example, the value -22425 may be converted to 2's-complement binary as follows.

    1. Take the positive value (22425) and subtract one (22424).

2. Represent this number in binary (0101 0111 1001 1000 = 0x5798).

3. Perform 1's (bitwise) complement (1010 1000 0110 0111 = 0xa867 = -22425).

For unsigned types, all bits, including the MSB, contribute to the magnitude of a positive number. Thus, unsigned variables may store values twice as large as signed variables of equivalent capacity. In the example above, the value of the bit-pattern for an unsigned type is 43111.

The C language has no mechanism to represent binary numbers directly, but provides ways to represent values in decimal, octal, and hexadecimal. For most purposes, decimal numbers are most convenient, but for bitwise operations, a hexadecimal representation is usually more appropriate. Hexadecimal (base 16) numbers effectively break binary values into blocks of four, making them easier to manage. With experience, hex tends to be more comprehensible than plain binary.

1.     **Bitwise Operators**

C provides six bitwise operators: AND &, OR |, exclusive OR (XOR) ", NOT ~, left-shift <<, and right-shift >>. These operators may be applied only to integer operands, char, short, int, and long, which may be signed or unsigned; they may not be used with floating-point operands. The &, |, ", <<, and >> operators each have corresponding assignment operators &=, |=, "=, <<=, and >>=. These behave analogously to the arithmetic assignment operators. For example,

    z &= x | y;

is equivalent to

    z = z & (x | y);

Important. As mentioned in Section 2.9, the bitwise operators, &, |, and ~, are different from the logical operators AND &&, OR ||, and NOT !, and should not be confused with them. These differences will be made clear in the discussion below.

1.     **AND, OR, XOR, and NOT**

The &, |, ", and ~ operators permit Boolean logic operations on individual bits. The ~ operator is a unary operator, which simply converts a 0 to 1 and vice-versa. The other three are binary operators, which compare two bits according to the rules in the following table.

| x y | x & y | x \| y | x " y |
|-----|-------|--------|-------|
| 0 0 0 | 0 | 0 | |
| 0 1 0 | 1 | 1 | |
| 1 0 0 | 1 | 1 | |
| 1. | 1 0 | | |

Consider the following 8-bit (1-byte) example. We define three unsigned variables

    unsigned char x = 55; /* 55 (dec) = 0x37 (hex) = 0011 0111 (binary). */
    unsigned char y = 25; /* 25 (dec) = 0x19 (hex) = 0001 1001 (binary). */
    unsigned char z;

and perform a series of operations on them, storing the result in z. The first, z = x & y, makes z equal to 17.

```
0011 0111 0001 1001 &
0001 0001    /* result is 17 (dec) = 0x11 (hex) */
```

The bitwise & (AND) operator sets a bit in z to 1 only if both corresponding bits in x and y are one. This operator is typically used to reset bits to zero and to select certain bits for testing.

The second operation, z = x | y, makes z equal to 63.

```
0011 0111
0001 1001
|
0011 1111    /* result is 63 (dec) = 0x3f (hex) */
```

The bitwise | (inclusive OR) operator sets a bit to 1 if either or both corresponding bits in x and y are one. It is typically used to set selected bits to one.

The third operation, z = x " y, makes z equal to 46.

```
0011 0111
0001 1001
~
1.   1110    /* result is 46 (dec) = 0x2e (hex) */
```

The bitwise " (exclusive OR) operator sets a bit to 1 if either, but not both, corresponding bits in x and y are one. It is typically used to toggle selected bits to the alternate state.

The fourth operation, z = ~x, makes z equal to 200.

```
1.   0111 ~
1100 1000    /* result is 200 (dec) = 0xc8 (hex) */
```

The bitwise ~ (one's complement) operator converts a 1 bit to 0 and a 0 bit to 1. It is commonly used to negate a group of bits, and is often used in conjunction with the shift operators.

## 1.      **Right Shift and Left Shift**

The shift operators, << and >>, shift the bits of an integer variable to the left or right, respectively. For a left-shift operation x << n, the bits in x are shifted n bit positions to the left, with the shifted-out bits being lost and the vacated bits being filled with zeros.

```
char x  = 0x19;    /*  Equals 0001 1001 binary (25 decimal).   */
char y  = x << 2;  /*  Equals 0110 0100 binary (100 decimal).  */
```

Shifting x by negative n, or by n greater than or equal to the width of x (in bits), results in an undefined value.

The right-shift operator is a little more complicated. If the variable x is unsigned, then x >> n behaves analogously to left-shift; the n right-most bits are shifted-out and the vacated bits are filled with zeros. However, if x is a signed variable, the expression is implementation dependent. Some machines perform "logical shift", which fills the vacated bits with zeros (as for unsigned right-shift), while others perform "arithmetic shift", which fills the vacated bits with the value of the sign bit. For example,

```
signed  char x  =-75;       /* Equals 1011 0101 binary. */
signed  char y  =x >> 2; /* Equals 0010 1101 if logical shift. */
                         /* Equals 1110 1101 if arithmetic shift. */
```

Thus, on a machine that performs logical right-shift, the value of y is 45, while on a machine that performs arithmetic right-shift, the value of y is -19. In general, it is usually preferred to use unsigned types for bitwise operations to avoid non-portable behaviour.

Notice that a left-shift by n is equivalent to multiplication by $2^n$ (e.g., $x << 2$ is equal to $x * 4$). Similarly, right-shift by n is equivalent to division by $2^n$. (More precisely, right-shift by n is equivalent to division by $2^n$ if the operand is unsigned or non-negative, or if the variable is negative and the machine performs arithmetic right-shift.) Bitwise operations are sometimes used to perform arithmetic expressions if the right-hand operand is a power of two. For example, the following expressions are equivalent.

| | | | | |
|---|---|---|---|---|
| x  * 2  is | equivalent | to | x << 1 |
| x  / 16 is | equivalent | to | x >> 4 |
| x  % 8  is | equivalent | to | x & 7 |

Bitwise expressions tend to be faster than integer arithmetic, but such optimisations are generally redundant as modern compilers will tend to replace "power of two" arithmetic with bitwise operations automatically.

1.      **Operator Precedence**

The precedence of the bitwise operators is lower than the arithmetic operators, with the exception of the unary ~ operator, which has equal precedence to the unary (logical) ! operator. The left and right shift operators have greater precedence than the relational operators < and >, but &, |, and " have lower precedence. The precedence of & is greater than ", which is greater than |. All bitwise operators have greater precedence than the logical operators && and ||.

   As with the arithmetic, relational and logical operators, it is unwise to rely on precedence in multi-operation expressions. Such practice tends to produce obscure and error-prone code. It is far better to make ones intent clear with parentheses.

1.      **Common Bitwise Operations**

Bitwise operations are commonly used for one of two purposes. The first is to conserve space by packing several variables into a single byte (e.g., binary "flags" that need only represent the values 0 or 1). The second is to interface with hardware, where a group of bits at a certain address correspond to the pins of some device. In both cases we want to be able to manipulate and test individual bits or groups of bits.

```
/* 0001 binary */ /* 0010 binary */ /* 0100 binary */ /* 1000 binary */ /* 1111 binary */
enum {
    FIRST = 0x01, SECND = 0x02, THIRD = 0x04, FORTH = 0x08, ALL = 0x0f
};
```

   The following example presents some common idioms for dealing with bits, which allow us to turn bits on or off and to test their current state. These techniques are collectively known as "masking" as they enable particular bits to be selected according to a specified *bit-mask*. The first step in creating a mask is to define variables to represent each bit of the integer variable; (we will consider only the lowest 4 bits in this, rather contrived, example).

The constants are each powers of two, so that just one bit is set and the rest are zeros. The exception is ALL, which defines a mask to select all four bits. An equivalent way to define the above constants is to use the left-shift operator as follows.

```
enum {
```

$$\text{FIRST} = 1 \leq 0 \; , $$
$$\text{SECND} = 1 \leq 1 \; , $$
$$\text{THIRD} \leq 2$$

```
         = 1     ≤   :
FORT          ≤   3
H = 1         ≤   :
                  (

                  :
                  :

ALL =         :
~(~           )
```

The last of these is a trifle cryptic, but is a common technique for creating a specified number of ones. The key is to realise that ~0 creates a value where all bits are 1's. For example, (assuming we are dealing with an 8-bit value)

1111 1111 /* ~0 */

1111 0000 /* ~0 << 4 */
0000 1111 /* ~(~0 << 4) */

The set of statements below depict a number of typical masking operations. By combining masks, we can select specific groups of bits to set, reset, or toggle, or to test as a conditional expression.

```
unsigned flags = 0;
flags |= SECOND | THIRD | FORTH;   /* Set bits 2,3,4    (1110)   */
flags &= '(FIRST | THIRD);         /* Reset bits 1,3    (1010)   */
flags "= THIRD | FORTH;            /* Toggle bits 3,4 (0110).    */
```

```
if ((flags & (FIRST | FORTH)) == 0) /* TRUE if bits 1 and 4 are off. */
    flags &= ~ALL;                  /* Reset all bits (0000). */
```

There are several points to note from this example. First, notice how the | operator is used to combine masks, and the ~ operator is used to negate this result so that all bits are one *except* the mask bits. Second, notice the use of the various assignment operators, which apply the masks to the left-hand operand, flags. The |= operator is used to set bits (i.e., turn bits on) and the &= operator is used to reset bits (i.e., turn bits off). These operations determine the state of the specified bits in flags regardless of their current state. On the other hand, the "= operator is used to toggle selected bits so that they become the opposite of their current state. Finally, notice in the second-last line how the bitwise operators can be used to create conditional expressions based on the state of particular bits. Individual bits, or groups of bits, may be selected via the & operator.

## 1.    Bit-fields

C provides an alternative to bit-masking operations for packing several objects into a single machine word. This facility is called a *bit-field*, and it uses structure syntax to define several objects within a single variable. Thus, the example from the previous section may have been represented as

```
struct {
    unsigned first : 1;
    unsigned secnd : 1;
    unsigned third : 1;
    unsigned forth : 1;
} flags;
```

This defines a variable flags that contains four 1-bit fields. The number following the colon represents the field width in bits. The individual fields are accessed in the same manner as structure members, so that individual bits may be manipulated as follows.

```
flags.secnd = flags.third = flags.forth = 1; flags.first = flags.third = 0;
flags.third = flags.third; flags.forth = flags.forth; if (flags.first == 0 &&
flags.forth == 0) flags.first = flags.secnd = flags.third = flags.forth = 0;
```

Notice that these operations perform the same basic tasks as the bit-masking code in the previous section.

To novice C programmers, bit-fields may seem a more natural representation than the previous bit-masking operations, but this is a superficial advantage and bit-fields should be used with caution.

The problem is that almost everything about bit-fields is implementation dependent and, without due care, they can promote non-portable code. For example, different machines apply different restrictions on field widths; some machines impose a maximum width of 16-bits while others permit 32-bits. Also, the way the fields are packed within the structure (i.e., their alignment) varies between machines. Byte-order dependencies are another issue.

In general, bitwise operations and masking are preferred over bit-fields. They permit direct control of bit packing and, with a little experience, the masking idioms tend to be more convenient for managing groups of bits. When needing to manipulate individual bits, additional convenience can be attained via a few choice macros, such as the following (obtained from bitops.h in the *Snippets* source repository, www.snippets.org).

```
#define  BitSet(arg,posn)  ((arg) |  (1L << (posn)))
#define  BitClr(arg,posn)  ((arg) &~(1L << (posn)))
#define  BitFlp(arg,posn)  ((arg) "  (1L << (posn)))
#define  BitTst(arg,posn)  ((arg) &  (1L << (posn)))
```

These macros set, reset, toggle, and test, respectively, the posn bit of variable arg. They might be used as in the examples below.

```
enum { FIRST, SECND, THIRD,
FORTH }; unsigned flags = 0;

flags = BitSet(flags, FIRST); /* Set first bit. */ flags =
BitFlp(flags, THIRD); /* Toggle third bit. */ if
(BitTst(flags, SECND) == 0) /* Test second bit. */ flags
= 0;
```

# Chapter 13

## Input and Output

The C language provides no direct facilities for input and output (IO), and, instead, these operations are supplied as functions in the standard library. This chapter describes the most commonly used functions. It also discusses the topic of command-shell redirection which, while non-standard, is widely supported, and the topic of command-line arguments, which enables a program to receive instructions from its calling environment.

It is important to realise that this chapter does not present all the functions related to IO in the standard library and, of the functions it does discuss, it does not cover every detail. More complete information can be found in, for example, [KR88, pages 241-248] and [HS95, pages 343-383].

### 1.     Formatted IO

The standard functions for formatted IO, printf() and scanf(), have been mentioned at a cursory level in previous chapters. These functions are very powerful and possess a level of sophistication beyond the scope of this text (although we will touch on these more complex aspects briefly). However, for most common purposes, they are intuitive, flexible and simple to use.

### 1.     Formatted Output: printf()

The function printf() is a general purpose print function that converts and formats its arguments to a character string, and prints the result to *standard output* (typically the screen). The general interface for printf() is

> int printf(const char *format, arg1, arg2, ... );

The first argument is a *format string,* which defines the layout of the printed text. This is followed by zero or more optional arguments, with the number of arguments, and their type, being determined by the contents of the format string. The return value is the number of characters printed, unless an error occurs during output whereupon the return value is EOF.

The format string is composed of ordinary characters and conversion specification characters. The former are printed verbatim, while the latter are used to control the conversion of the optional arguments following the format string. Conversion specifications are identified by a % character followed by a number of optional fields and terminated by a type conversion character. A simple example is

> printf("%d green %s sitting on a wall.\n", 10, "bottles");

where the ordinary characters "green" and "sitting on a wall.\n" are printed verbatim, and the conversion specifiers %d and %s insert the additional arguments at the appropriate locations. The type conversion character must match its associated argument type; in the example, the %d indicates an integer argument and the %s indicates a string argument.

There are different conversion characters for ints (d, i, o, x, c), unsigned ints (u), doubles (f, e, g), strings (s), and pointers (p). Details of these may be found in any C reference text. To print a % character, the conversion specification %% is used.

Between the % and the type conversion character there may exist a number of optional fields. These control the formatting of the converted argument. Consider, for example, the conversion specifier %-#012.4hd (this example is from [HS95, page 368]).

The first field is a set of flags, which modify the meaning of the conversion operation (e.g., make the argument left-justified, or pad with zeros). The second field specifies a minimum width reserved for the converted argument (in characters), and so provides padding for under-sized values. The third field is a precision specification, which has various different meanings for integers, floating point values and strings. The fourth field is a size modifier, which indicates conversion to a longer or shorter type than the default conversion types (where the default types are, for example, int or double).

Again, a good reference text will have more information regarding these conversion specifications. Most often printf() involves just the % and a conversion character, and rarely get more complex than the following example,

```
printf("Value = %-10.3f radians.\n", fval);
```

which, if passed the floating point value 3.14159, would print

```
Value = 3.142      radians.
```

where the converted floating point value is left-justified (due to the - flag), is padded with sufficient space for 10 characters, and displays 3 digits after the decimal point.

It is essential that the type conversion specifier matches the type of the argument, as the compiler cannot catch type-mismatches for variable-length argument lists. However, there is no need for conversion characters for types float and short, etc, as these types are automatically converted to double and int, respectively, by the usual argument promotion rules.[1]

Aside. The ability of write functions with variable-length argument lists is not restricted to im- plementers of the standard library. The standard provides facilities that enable application programmers to write functions with these same capabilities. The standard header stdarg.h contains a set of macro definitions that define how to step through an argument list. The declaration of a variable-length argument list is marked by ellipsis ( ... ) in the function interface, and typically the type and number of arguments is specified using a format string, as in the following example.

```
int varfunc(char *format, ...);
```

Note, the ellipsis declaration may only appear at the end of an argument list. The implementation of such functions using the macros from stdarg.h is beyond the scope of this text.

1.    **Formatted Input: scanf()**

The scanf() function is the input analog of printf(), providing many of the same conversion specifications in the opposite direction (although there are differences, so be wary). It obtains data from *standard input,* which is typically the keyboard. The general interface for scanf() is

```
int scanf(const char *format, ...);
```

This is identical to printf() in form, with a format string and a variable argument list, but an important difference is that the arguments for scanf() must be pointer types. This allows the input data to be stored at the address designated by the pointer using pass-by-reference semantics. For example,

```
double fval;
scanf("%lf", fval); /* Wrong */
scanf("%lf", &fval); /* Correct, store input in fval. */
```

scanf() reads characters from standard input and interprets them according to the format string specification. It stops when it exhausts the format string, or when some input fails to match a conversion specification. Its return value is the number of values successfully assigned in its variable-length argument list. If a conflict occurs between the a conversion specification and the actual input, the character causing the conflict is left unread and is processed by the next standard input operation.

The mechanics of the format string and its conversion specifications are even more complicated for scanf() than for printf(), and there are many details and caveats that will not be discussed here. Most of the conversion characters for printf()—d, i, o, x, c, u, f, e, g, s, p, etc—have similar meanings for scanf(), but there are certain differences, some subtle. Thus, one should not use the documentation for one as a guide for the other. Some of these differences are as follows.

- Where printf() has four optional fields, scanf() has only two. It has the width and size modifier fields but not the flags and precision fields.

- For printf() the width field specifies a *minimum* reserve of space (i.e., padding), while for scanf() it defines a *maximum* limit on the number of characters to be read.

- An asterisk character (*) may be used in place of the width field for both printf() and scanf(), but with different meanings. For printf() it allows the width field to be determined by an additional argument, but for scanf() it suppresses assignment of an input value to its argument.

- The conversion character [ is not valid for printf(), but for scanf() it permits a *scanset* of characters to be specified, which allows scanf() to control exactly the characters it reads in.

- The size modifier field is typically neglected for printf(), but is vital for scanf(). For example, to read a float, one uses the conversion specifier %f. To read a double, the size modifier l (for long) must appear, /1f.

Of the above, the third and fourth points are rather advanced features that we will not dwell on further. However, the last point is important, and a common source of errors for new C programmers. The conversion specifier and size modifier *must* match the associated argument type or the result is undefined.

The scanf() format string consists of conversion specifiers, ordinary characters, and white-space. Where ordinary characters appear in the format string, they must match exactly the format of the input. For example, the following statement is used to read a date of the form dd/mm/yy.

```
int day, month, year;
scanf("%d/%d/%d", &day, &month, &year);
```

In general scanf() ignores white-space characters in its format string, and skips over white-space in stdin as it looks for input values. Exceptions to this rule arise with the %c and %[ conversion specifiers, which do not skip white-space. For example, if the user types in "one two" for each of the statements below, they will obtain different results.

```
char s[10], c;
scanf("%s%c", s, &c); /* s = "one", c = ' ' */
scanf("%s %c", s, &c); /* s = "one", c = 't' */
```

In the first case, the %c reads in the next character after %s leaves off, which is a space. In the second, the white-space in the format string causes scanf() to consume any white-space after "one", leaving the first non-space character (t) to be assigned to c.

While the many details of scanf() formatting complicates a complete understanding, its basic use is quite simple. Rarely does an input statement get more complicated than

```
short a; double b; char c[20];
scanf("%hd %lf %s", &a, &b, c);
```

However, it is worth noting that the above form of string (%s) input is not ideal. A string is read up to the first white-space character unless terminated early by a width field. Thus, a very long input of consecutive non-space characters may overflow the string's character buffer. To prevent overflow, a string conversion specification should always include a width field. Consider a situation where a user types in the words "small supererogatory" for the following input code.

```
char s1[10], s2[10], s3[10]; scanf("%9s %9s
%9s", s1, s2, s3);
```

Notice the width fields are one-less than the array sizes to allow room for the terminating \0. The first word "small" fits into s1, but the second word is over-long—its first nine characters "supererog" are placed in s2 and the rest "atory" goes into s3.

A few final warnings about scanf(). First, keep in mind that the arguments in its variable length argument list *must* be pointers; forgetting the & in front of non-pointer variables is a very common mistake. Second, when there is a conflict between a conversion specification and the actual input, the offending character is left unread. Thus, an expression like

```
while (scanf("%d", &val) != EOF)
```

is dangerous as it will loop forever if there is a conflict. Third, while scanf() is a good choice when the exact format of the input is known, other input techniques may be better suited if the format may vary. For example, the combination of fgets() and sscanf(), described in the next section, is a useful alternative if the input format is not precisely known. The fgets() function reads a line of characters into a buffer, and sscanf() extracts the data, and can pick out different parts using multiple passes if necessary.

1.    **String Formatting**

The functions sprintf() and sscanf() perform essentially the same operations as printf() and scanf(), respectively, but, rather than interact with stdout or stdin, they operate on a character array argument. They present the following interfaces.

```
int sprintf(char *buf, const char *format, ...); int
sscanf(const char *buf, const char *format, ...);
```

The sprintf() function stores the resulting formatted string in buf and automatically appends this string with a terminating \0 character. It returns the number of characters stored (excluding \0). This function is very useful for a wide range of string manipulation operations. For example, the following code segment creates a format string at runtime, which prevents scanf() from overflowing its character buffer.

```
char buf[100], format[10];
sprintf(format, "%%%ds", sizeof(buf)-1); /* Create format string "%99s". */
scanf(format, buf);                       /* Get string from stdin. */
```

The input string is thus limited to not more than 99 characters plus 1 for the terminating \0.

sscanf() extracts values from the string buf according to the format string, and stores the results in the additional argument list. It behaves just like scanf() with buf replacing stdin as the source of input characters. An attempt to read beyond the end of string buf for sscanf() is equivalent to reaching the end-of-file for scanf(). The sscanf() function is often used in conjunction with a line input function, such as fgets(), as in the following example.

```
char buf[100]; double dval;
fgets(buf, sizeof(buf), stdin); /* Get a line of input, store in buf. */ sscanf(buf, "%lf",
&dval);                          /* Extract a double from buf. */
```

## 13.2 File IO

The C language is closely tied to the UNIX operating system; they were initially developed in parallel, and UNIX was implemented in C. Thus, much of the standard C library is modelled on UNIX facilities, and in particular the way it performs input and output by reading or writing to files.

*In the UNIX operating system, all input and output is done by reading or writing files, because all peripheral devices, even keyboard and screen, are files in the file system. This means that a single homogeneous interface handles all communication between a program and peripheral devices [KR88, page 169].*

1.    **Opening and Closing Files**

A file is referred to by a FILE pointer, where FILE is a structure declaration defined with a typedef in header stdio.h.[7] This file pointer "points to a structure that contains information about the file, such as the location of a buffer, the current character position in the buffer, whether the file is being read or written, and whether errors or end-of-file have occurred" [KR88, page 160]. All these implementation details are hidden from users of the standard library via the FILE type-name and the associated library functions.

A file is opened by the function fopen(), which has the interface

```
FILE *fopen(const char *name, const char *mode);
```

The first argument, name, is a character string containing the name of the file. The second is a mode string, which determines how the file may be used. There are three basic modes: read "r", write "w" and append "a". The first opens an existing file for reading, and fails if the file does not exist. The other two open a file for writing, and create a new file if it does not already exist. Opening an existing file in "w" mode, first clears the file of its existing data (i.e., overwrites the existing file). Opening in "a" mode preserves the existing data and adds new data to the end of the file.

Each of these modes may include an additional "update" specification signified by a + character (i.e., "r+", "w+", "a+"), which enables the file stream to be used for both input and output. This ability is most useful in conjunction with the *random access* file operations described in Section 13.2.4 below.

Some operating systems treat "binary" files differently to "text" files. (For example, UNIX handles binary and text files the same; Win32 represents them differently.) The standard C library caters for this variation by permitting a file to be explicitly marked as binary with the addition of a b character to the file-open mode (e.g., "rb" opens a binary file for reading).

If opening a file is successful, fopen() returns a valid FILE * pointer. If there is an error, it returns NULL (e.g., attempting to open a file for reading that does not exist, or attempting to open a file without appropriate permissions). As with other functions that return pointers to limited resources, such as the dynamic memory allocation functions, it is prudent to always check the return value for NULL.

To close a file, the file pointer is passed to fclose(), which has the interface

    int fclose(FILE *fp);

This function breaks the connection with the file and frees the file pointer. It is good practice to free file pointers when a file is no longer needed as most operating systems have a limit on the number of files that a program may have open simultaneously. However, fclose() is called automatically for each open file when a program terminates.

1.      **Standard IO**

When a program begins execution, there are three text streams predefined and open. These are standard input (stdin), standard output (stdout) and standard error (stderr). The first two signify "normal" input and output, and for most interactive environments are directed to the keyboard and screen, respectively. Their input and output streams are usually buffered, which means that characters are accumulated in a queue and sent in packets, minimising expensive system calls. Buffering may be controlled by the standard function setbuf(). The stderr stream is reserved for sending error messages. Like stdout it is typically directed to the screen, but its output is unbuffered.

1.      **Sequential File Operations**

Once a file is opened, operations on the file—reading or writing—usually negotiate the file in a sequential manner, from the beginning to the end. The standard library provides a number of different operations for sequential IO.

The simplest functions process a file one character at a time. To write a character there are the functions

    int fputc(int c, FILE *fp); int putc(int c,
    FILE *fp); int putchar(int c);

where calling putchar(c) is equivalent to calling putc(c, stdout). The functions putc() and fputc() are identical, but putc() is typically implemented as a macro for efficiency. These functions return the character that was written, or EOF if there was an error (e.g., the hard disk was full).

To read a character, there are the functions

    int fgetc(FILE *fp); int getc(FILE *fp); int
    getchar(void);

which are analogous to the character output functions. Calling getchar() is equivalent to calling getc(stdin), and getc() is usually a macro implementation of fgetc().[8] These functions return the next character in the character stream unless either the end-of-file is reached or an error occurs. In these anomalous cases, they return EOF. It is possible to push a character c back onto an input stream using the function

    int ungetc(int c, FILE *fp);

The pushed back character will be read by the next call to getc() (or getchar() or fscanf(), etc) on that stream.

Note. The symbolic constant EOF is returned by standard IO functions to signal either end-of-file or an IO error. For input functions, it may be necessary to determine which of these cases is being flagged. Two standard functions, feof() and ferror(), are provided for this task and, respectively, they return non-zero if the prior EOF was due to end-of-file or an output error.

Formatted IO can be performed on files using the functions

int fprintf(FILE *fp, const char *format, ...); int
fscanf(FILE *fp, const char *format, ...);

These functions are generalisations of printf() and scanf(), which are equivalent to the calls fprintf(stdout, format, ...) and fscanf(stdin, format, ...), respectively.

Characters can be read from a file a line at a time using the function

char *fgets(char *buf, int max, FILE *fp);

which reads at most max-1 characters from the file pointed to by fp and stores the resulting string in buf. It automatically appends a \0 character to the end of the string. The function returns when it encounters a \n character (i.e., a newline), or reaches the end-of-file, or has read the maximum number of characters. It returns a pointer to buf if successful, and NULL for end-of-file or if there was an error.

Character strings may be written to a file using the function

int fputs(const char *str, FILE *fp);

which returns a non-negative value if successful and EOF if there was an error. Note, the string need not contain a \n character, and fputs() will not append one, so strings may be written to the same line with successive calls.

For reading and writing binary files, a pair of functions are provided that enable objects to be passed to and from files directly without first converting them to a character string. These functions are

size_t fread(void *ptr, size_t size, size_t nobj, FILE *fp); size_t
fwrite(const void *ptr, size_t size, size_t nobj, FILE *fp);

and they permit objects of any type to be read or written, including arrays and structures. For example, if a structure called Astruct were defined, then an array of such structures could be written to file as follows.

struct Astruct mystruct[10]; fwrite(&mystruct, sizeof(Astruct), 10, fp);

1.    **Random Access File Operations**

The previous file IO functions progress through a file sequentially. The standard library also provides a means to move back and forth within a file to any specified location. These file positioning functions are

long ftell(FILE *fp);
int fseek(FILE *fp, long offset, int from); void rewind(FILE *fp);

The first, ftell(), returns the current position in the file stream. For binary files this value is the number of characters preceding the current position. For text files the value is implementation defined. In both cases the value is in a form suitable for the second argument of fseek(), and the value 0L represents the beginning of the file.

The second function, fseek(), sets the file position to a location specified by its second argument. This parameter is an offset, which shifts the file position relative to a given reference location. The reference location is given by the third argument and may be one of three values as defined by the symbolic constants SEEK_SET, SEEK_CUR, and SEEK_END. These specify the beginning of the file, the current file position, and the end of file, respectively. Having shifted the file position via fseek(), a subsequent read or write will proceed from this new position.

For binary files, fseek() may be used to move the file position to any chosen location. For text files, however, the set of valid operations is restricted to the following.

fseek(fp, 0L, SEEK_SET); fseek(fp, 0L, SEEK_CUR); fseek(fp, 0L, SEEK_END); fseek(fp, pos, SEEK_SET);
/* Move to beginning of file. */
/* Move to current location (no effect). */ /* Move to end of file. */
/* Move to pos. */

In the last case, the value pos must be a position returned by a previous call to ftell(). Binary files, on the other hand, permit more arbitrary use, such as

fseek(fp, -4L, SEEK_CUR); /* Move back 4 bytes. */

The program below shows an example of ftell() and fseek() to determine the length of a file in bytes. The file itself may be plain text, but it is opened as binary so that ftell() returns the number of characters to the end-of-file.

```
1. /* Compute the length of a file in bytes. From Snippets (ansiflen.c) */
2. long flength(char *fname)
3. {
4.
        long length
        = — 1L;
        FILE *fptr;

        fptr =
        fopen(fname,
        "rb"); if (fptr !=
        NULL) {
                fseek(fptr, 0L,
                SEEKEND);
                length = ftell(fptr);
                fclose(fptr);
        }
        return length;
}
```

The third function, rewind(), returns the position to the beginning of the file. Calling rewind(fp) is equivalent to the statement fseek(fp, 0L, SEEK_SET).

Two other file positioning functions are available in the standard library: fgetpos() and fsetpos(). These perform essentially the same tasks as ftell() and fseek(), respectively, but are able to handle files too large for their positions to be representable by a long integer.

1.      **Command-Shell Redirection**

Often programs are executed from a command-interpreter environment (also called a shell). Most operating systems possess such an interpreter. For example, Win32 has a DOS-shell and UNIX-like systems have various similar shell environments such as the C-shell, the Bourne-shell, the Korn-shell, etc. Most shells facilitate redirection of stdin and stdout using the commands < and >, respectively. Redirection is not part of the C language, but an operating system service that supports the C input- output model.

```
#include <stdio.h>
```

```
/* Write stdin to stdout */
int main(void)
{
        int c;
        while ((c = getchar())
            != EOF)
            putchar(c);
}
```

Consider the example program above. It simply reads characters from stdin and forwards them to stdout. Normally this means the characters typed at the keyboard are echoed on the screen after the user hits the "enter" key. Assume the program executable is named "repeat". repeat
    type some text 123 type some
    text 123

However, a file may be substituted for the keyboard by redirection.
    repeat <infile.txt
    display contents of infile.txt

Alternatively, a file may be substituted for the screen, or for both keyboard and screen as in the following example, which copies the contents of infile.txt to outfile.txt. repeat <infile.txt >outfile.txt

Further redirection commands are >> and |. The former redirects stdout but, unlike >, appends the redirected output rather than overwriting the existing file contents. The latter is called a "pipe", and it directs the stdout of one program to the stdin of another. For example,
    prog1 | prog2
prog1 executes first and its stdout is accumulated in a temporary buffer and, once the program has terminated, prog2 executes with this set of output as its stdin.
    The stderr stream is not redirected, and so will still print messages to the screen even if stdout is redirected.


1.      **Command-Line Arguments**

The C language provides a mechanism for a program to obtain input parameters from the environment in which it executes. These are termed "command-line arguments" and are passed to the program when it begins execution. Until now we have specified the interface of main() as

        int main(void)

which is one of the two interfaces permitted by the ISO C standard. The other consists of two arguments

        int main(int argc, char *argv[])

where argc stands for *argument count* and argv stands for *argument vector.*

Style Note. The two parameters, of course, do not have to be named argc and argv, but this is a long-standing convention and should be upheld to assist code readability.

    The value of argc is the number of command-line parameters passed to the program upon execution. The parameter argv is a pointer to an array of character strings, where each string is one of the passed command-line parameters. The length of this array is argc+1 and the end element, argv[argc] is NULL. The value of argc is always at least one, as argv[0] is the name by which the program was invoked. If argc equals one, then there are no command-line arguments after the program name.

Consider the example program below. This program simply takes the set of command-line strings referred to by argv and prints them to stdout. We will assume the program executable is named "echo".

```
#include <stdio.h>

/* Print command-line arguments to stdout. */
int main (int argc, char *argv[])
{
    int i;
    for (i =1; i < argc;
    +—+i) printf("%s ",
    argv[i]); printf ("\n");
}
```

When a program is invoked from a command-line, each white-space separated string of characters including the program name becomes a command-line argument. Thus, typing

echo one two three 123

stores the strings "echo", "one", "two", "three" and "123" in locations referred to by argv[0] to argv[4], respectively, and argc is equal to five. This program then prints all arguments except argv[0]. Note, redirection commands do not appear as command-line arguments, so

echo one >outfile.txt two three 123

will print

one two three 123 in the file named

outfile.txt.

## Chapter 14

## Generic Programming

Writing generic and reusable software is one of the pinnacles of software design. It permits the creation of a toolbox of generally useful code modules or libraries that may be used time and again.

The antithesis of generic design is a set of functions that possess virtually identical code, but differ in terms of the types they operate on. The basic purpose of generic programming is to avoid such code repetition; to define an algorithm or data-structure and that works with a variety of different types. Coding for the general case tends to reduce the overall coding effort, reduce the likelihood of errors, and increase code modularity and reuse.

Some of the topics presented below have been covered in previous chapters. This chapter brings them together under the guise of writing generic programs. The most powerful feature in the C language for generic programming is the ability to cast between different types, particularly pointer types, and, most significantly, the generic pointer type void*. This chapter examines the use of void* in generic software design in terms of two examples: an expandable array and the standard library function qsort(). The discussion of qsort() also shows how function pointers can be used to enhance the flexibility of a generic design.

## 1. Basic Generic Design: Typedefs, Macros, and Unions

Typedefs, macros, and unions facilitate limited forms of generality, with each permitting increased flexibility in a specific area of code design. Typedefs provide type-name synonyms, macros circumvent C type-checking, and unions define variant types.

## 1. Typedefs

The keyword typedef permits the creation of new type names for existing types. These *type synonyms* permit an algorithm to be written such that it can work with different types by simply changing the appropriate typedefs. For example, by defining the name

typedef char Item;

an algorithm defined in terms of Item can be changed to work with doubles by simply changing the typedef to

typedef double Item;

This technique is demonstrated in the expandable vector example in Section 11.7, where the variable type contained by the vector is specified by a typedef.

The limitation of typedef is that its type is fixed at compile time, and an algorithm cannot be used with different types in a single program.

## 1. Macros

Macros can be used with different types in a given program because they avoid the type-constraints of the C compiler. The C preprocessor expands macro text inline, so that macros essentially automate code duplication. For example, given the macro

#define MAX(x,y) ((x)<(y) ? (y) : (x))

and a set of variables

int x = 1, y = 2, z; double a = 3.2, b = -9.1, c;

then the following code

z = MAX(x,y); c = MAX(a / 2.7,b + 1);

expands to

z = ((x)<(y) ? (y) : (x));
c = ((a / 2.7)<(b + 1) ? (b + 1) : (a / 2.7));

As another example, the macro below returns the number of elements in an array x.

#define NELEMS(x) (sizeof(x)/sizeof(x[0]))

This macro works for arrays of any type including arrays of doubles, pointers, structures, and so forth.

Using macros for anything but the most trivial of operations is not advised. To compose any significant algorithm as a macro is both notationally inconvenient and error prone. Macros do not obey the type and scope rules imposed by the C language, and can introduce cryptic syntactical errors if not used with caution.

1. **Unions**

Unions permit the definition of *variant* types—types that may represent one of several different types. This facility is useful if one wishes to pass various types at different times through the same function interface. It is also used to create a collection of different types (i.e., to create a heterogeneous array).

An example of a heterogeneous array is given in Section 11.8, where we noted that unions are usually wrapped in a structure, which defines the type of the value currently stored by the union. The following example shows a similar design for passing variant types to a function.

```c
enum VariantType { INT, FLOAT, STRING };

typedef struct {
    enum VariantType
    type; union {
        int i;
        float
        f;
        char
        *s;
    } value;
} Variant;

void interpret_command(Variant command)
{
    switch (command.type)
    {
        case     printf("Got      integer      %d\n",      break
        INT:     command.value.i);
        case     printf("Got         float      %f\n",      break
        FLOAT:                    command.val
                 ue.f);
        case     printf    ("Got    string    %s\n",    break
        STRING                     command.val
        :        ue.s);
        default: printf   ("Unknown   type   %d\n",    break
                 command.type);
    }
}
```

The function interpret_command() might be passed information as follows.

```c
Variant v, w;

i. type = INT;   v.value.i = -5;
w. type = STRING; w.value.s = "COMMAND";

interpret_command(v);
interpret_command(w);
```

Aside. Notice that the definition of the structure Variant (lines 3 to 10) contains an *unnamed* union type with a single variable value. Structures and unions do not have to be named if they define a set of variables and are never referred to again.

# 1.     **Advanced Generic Design: void \***

The void* pointer type, in conjunction with the ability to cast between pointer types, permits a very powerful and flexible form of generic programming. With these facilities we can implement algorithms and data-structures that operate on any number of different types. In addition, we show how function pointers can be used to specialise certain parts of an algorithm at run-time.

    This discussion is presented in terms of two examples. The first is the expandable array Vector that has been developed in Sections 9.5 and 11.7. The second is the standard library function qsort(), which is used to sort the elements of an array.

# 1.     **Case Study: Expandable Array**

The following implementation of the expandable array overcomes the limitations of the previous versions. It permits any number of Vector objects to be defined, and each of these may contain elements of a different type. There is no longer the constraint of one item-type per program that was imposed by typedef. This increase in flexibility comes at the price of a slight decrease in efficiency and a significant loss of compile-time type-safety. However, the issue of type-safety can be redeemed somewhat by using wrapper functions, as we shall see.

    The first thing to notice when reading this source code is how similar it is to the original implementation, which permitted just one vector and could only contain integers (see Section 9.5). A fully generic implementation is thus possible without any great increase in code complexity.

    The code below shows the contents of the public interface declared in vector.h. The header exports all the declarations that should be visible to the client in order to use this module. Notice that the definition of struct Vector is not exported. All operations on Vector are performed by its associated functions, and the client only ever uses a pointer as a handle to a Vector object. Particularly, the client never has access to the structure members. Therefore, only the structure *declaration,* which is called an "incomplete type" or "opaque type", needs to be visible to the client.

```
typedef struct Vector { void *begin; void *end; void *last; size_t itemsize;
} Vector;
/* pointer /* pointer /* pointer /* size of
    #ifndef
    GENERIC_EXPANDABLE_VECTO
    R_H   #define
    GENERIC_EXPANDABLE_VECTO
    R_H

    #include <stddef.h> /* for size_t */
    typedef struct Vector Vector;

    /* Vector creation and destruction. */
    Vector *vector_create(size_t
    capacity, size_t itemsize); void
    vector_destroy (Vector *v);

    /* Vector access operations. */
```

```
int vector_push_back( Vector *v,
const void *item); void
vector_pop_back( Vector *v, void
*item); void* vector_get_element
(Vector *v, size_t index); void*
vector_get_begin(Vector *v); void*
vector_get_end(Vector *v);

/* Size operations. */
size_t vector_get_item_size(const
Vector *v); size_t
vector_get_size(const Vector *v);
size_t vector_get_capacity (const
Vector *v); int
    vector_set_size(Vector *v, size_t
size);
int  vector_set_capacity(Vector *v, size_t size);

#endif
```

The next section of code is from the top of the source file vector.c. Lines 6 to 14 comprise the private interface, which contains implementation details that are internal to the Vector functionality and are hidden from the client.

```
#include <stdlib.h>
#include <string.h>
#include <assert.h>
#include "vector.h"

static const size_t StartSize = 5;  /* initial vector capacity */
static const float GrowthRate = 1.6f; /* geometric growth of vector capacity */

typedef struct Vector {
        void *data;          /* pointer to vector elements */
        size_t capacity;    /* current reserved memory for vector */
        size_t size;         /* current size of vector (number of stored items) */
        size_t itemsize;    /* size of each item */
        } Vector;
```

The next two functions create and destroy a Vector, respectively. Their implementation is trivial. The function vector_create() is passed two variables. The first is an initial capacity—the number of elements for which to allocate space. The second is the size of each element which, because the function is generic, is not known to the compiler and must be stated explicitly. For example, to create a Vector of integers with initial space for five values, we write

```
Vector v;
v = vector_create(5, sizeof(int));

Vector *vector_create(size_t capacity, size_t itemsize)
/* Initialise a vector with the specified capacity for items of size itemsize. */
{
        Vector *v = (Vector
        *)malloc(sizeof(Vector)); if (v) {
                v—>data = malloc(capacity*itemsize);
                v—>capacity = (v—>data == NULL) ? 0 : capacity;
```

```c
            v—>size = 0;
            v—> itemsize = itemsize;
    }
    return v;
}


void vector_destroy(Vector *v)
/* Release memory owned by vector. */
{
        free(v— >data); free(v);
}
```

The functions below provide access to the elements of Vector. Of these, the implementation of vector_push_back() is the most complex, but it is described thoroughly in Section 9.5. The only new features are the conversions between void* and char* pointer types, and the use of the standard library function memcpy() (see line 49).

```c
/* Return pointer to the element at the specified index. */
{
        assert(index >= 0 && index < v—
        >size); return (char*)v—>data +
        index * v—>itemsize;
}
```

```c
/* Return pointer to beginning of array (ie, to first element of
array). */ void* vector_get_begin(Vector *v) { return v—>data; }
```

```c
/* Return pointer to one-past-end of array. */
void* vector_get_end(Vector *v) { return (char*)v—>data + v—>size*v—>itemsize;
}
```

The final set of functions shown below are provided for completeness. Their implementations present no new details not described previously.

```c
/* Inquire after size of vector item. */
size_t vector_get_item_size(const Vector *v) { return v—>itemsize; }
```

```c
/* Inquire after vector size and capacity */
size_t vector_get_size(const Vector *v) { return v—>size; }
size_t vector_get_capacity(const Vector *v) { return v—>capacity; }
```

```c
int vector_set_size(Vector *v, size_t size)
/* Set vector size. Return 0 if successful, -1 if fails. */
{
        if (size > v—>capacity) {
                void *p = realloc(v—>data,
                size*v—>itemsize); if (p ==
                NULL)
                        return —1;

                v—>capacity = size; /* allocate succeeds, update
                data-structure */ v—>data = p;
        }

        v—>size = size;
        return 0;
}
```

```
int vector_set_capacity(Vector *v, size_t size)
/* Shrink or grow allocated memory reserve for array.
 * A size of 0 deletes the array. Return 0 if successful, -1 if fails. */
{
    if (size != v—>capacity) {
        void *p = realloc(v—>data, size*v—
>itemsize); if (p == NULL && size > 0)
            return —1;

        v—>capacity = size; v—>data = p;
    }

    if (size < v—>size)
        v—>size = size;
    return 0;
}
```

# 1.      **Type Specific Wrapper Functions**

The generic interface described above is sufficient for use in client applications, but is subject to a number of disadvantages. The most important is loss of type-safety. For example, having created a Vector of ints, the compiler will not prevent you from pushing doubles onto it, or attempting to pop char pointers. A related problem is that the compiler will not perform the usual type conversions when passing variables to these functions, such as converting a float to double for a Vector of doubles. And finally, this interface does not allow constants or expressions to be passed to a Vector, as in the following examples.

```
vector_push_back(v, &50);        /* Invalid, cannot take address of a constant. */
vector_push_back(v, &(i + j)); /* Invalid, cannot take address of an expression. */
```

A good technique to improve type-safety, and also address the other problems mentioned above, is to wrap the generic interface in type-specific "wrapper functions". These functions use the generic implementations to perform the bulk of the algorithm but provide interfaces that permit type checking and type conversion by the compiler. Consider the following set of wrapper functions for Vectors of type int. The header file vector_int.h contains the public interface.

```
#ifndef INT_EXPANDABLE_VECTOR_H_ #define
INT_EXPANDABLE_VECTOR_H_

#include "vector.h"

/* Vector creation. */
Vector *vector_create_int(size_t capacity);

/* Vector access operations. */
int vector_push_back_int(Vector *v, int item); int vector_pop_back_int(Vector *v);

#endif
```

There are several points to note from this header file. The first is operations such as pushing an integer onto the array may be performed with expressions or constants.

```
vector_push_back_int(v, 50); vector_push_back_int(v, i + j);
```

The second is that items of the wrong type are automatically converted to ints by the usual type conversion rules.

```
char val = 32;
vector_push_back_int(v, val); /* val automatically converted to int. */
```

Finally, notice that wrappers are not provided for most of the generic public interface. This is because most operations do not require a type-specific wrapper, and the generic interface can be used directly without issue. For example, vector_destroy(), vector_get_element(), vector_set_size(), etc, do not rely on type information.

Style Note. It is good practice to avoid including header files in other header files where possible. This is in order to minimise dependencies between different modules. In the case of vector_int.h, the inclusion of vector.h could be avoided, and replaced with

```
typedef struct Vector Vector;
```

as the declarations in vector_int.h make no reference to any other part of the Vector public interface. Rather, vector.h would be included in the source file vector_int.c, and the dependence between the two headers is reduced to a single declaration.

We have chosen to include vector.h in vector_int.h on this occasion because the two modules are inherently coupled. We never call vector_create_int() without calling the generic function vector_destroy(). Thus, there is no need to minimise their dependence.

The next set of functions are the contents of the source file vector_int.c. These functions call the generic functions to perform the actual operations, but also incorporate some type-checking code. In the following implementations, checking is very primitive—simply that the passed vector contains items of the appropriate size, which protects against memory errors. They do not check whether the actual element types are correct, and different types of compatible size will not be caught. It is possible to strengthen this type-checking by including a type-field in the Vector structure similar to that used for unions in Section 14.1.3.

```
#include "vector_int.h" #include <assert.h>

Vector *vector_create_int(size_t capacity)
{
    return vector_create(capacity, sizeof(int));
}

int vector_push_back_int(Vector *v, int item)
{
    assert(vector_get_item_size(v)
    == sizeof (int)); return
    vector_push_back(v, &item);
}

int vector_pop_back_int(Vector *v)
{
    int i;
    assert(vector_get_item_size(v)
    == sizeof (int));
    vector_pop_back(v, &i); return
```

1.       **Case Study: qsort()**

The standard library function qsort() is declared in header stdlib.h and provides a generic algorithm for sorting arrays. The function is called qsort() because it is typically implemented using the algorithm known as "quick-sort". Quick-sort is the algorithm of choice for most sorting tasks, as it is on average the fastest general-purpose method available. The details and pitfalls of quick-sort are beyond the scope of this text but are discussed thoroughly in any good algorithms textbook.

The qsort() function is interesting, not simply because it can be used with arrays of any type, but because it uses function pointers to allow the client to customise part of the sorting algorithm. The ability to create specialised sub-algorithms via function pointers greatly enhances the power of generic code. In the case of qsort(), the custom sub-algorithm is a comparison function that compares two elements in an array so that they might be placed in sorted order.

The general interface of qsort() is

        void qsort(void *array, size_t nobj, size_t size,
                    int (*cmp)(const void *, const void *));

where the first three arguments are a pointer to the beginning of an array, the number of elements in the array, and the size of each element, respectively. The last argument is a pointer to a comparison function, which takes two (generic) arguments and returns an integer. This function is used internally by qsort(), which passes it pairs of array elements. The function returns a negative value if the first element is less than the second, a positive value if the second is less than the first, and zero if they are equal.

The following example uses qsort() to sort an array of structures of type struct Database. This structure contains two values—a key and another item—and the array elements are to be sorted so that the keys are in ascending order. The function comp_dbase(), in lines 12 to 23, specifies this ordering given any two Database variables, and is the custom comparison function for qsort(). Notice that the comparison statements on lines 18 to 22 may have been written more succinctly as

        return d1->key - d2->key;

but we refrain from this approach as the result might overflow if one key is very negative and the other very positive.

In main() we first create an array of Database elements, and give each element a random key value (lines 30 to 33). We then sort the array and print the result with the keys now in ascending order.

```
#include <stdlib.h>
#include <string.h>
#include <stdio.h>

#define NELEMS(x) (sizeof(x)/sizeof(x[0]))

struct Database { int key; float item;
};

int comp_dbase(const void *a, const void *b)
/* Returns -ve if a<b, 0 if a==b, +ve if a>b */
{
        struct Database *d1 = (struct
```

```c
    Database *)a; struct Database *d2
    = (struct Database *)b;

    if (d1->key < d2->key)
        return -1;
    if (d1->key > d2->key)
        retu
rn 1;
    return 0;
}

int main(void)
{
    int i;
    struct Database db[10];

    for (i = 0; i < NELEMS(db); ++i) {
        db[i].key = rand(); db[i].item
        = (float)i;
    }

    qsort(db, NELEMS(db), sizeof db[0], comp_dbase);

    for (i = 0; i < NELEMS(db); ++i)
        printf("7,5d    db[i].key, db[i].item);
}
```

The power of qsort() is that it may be used with arrays of any arbitrary data-type such as,

```c
struct Dictionary { char *word; char *defn;
};
```

and each different data type may be compared via its own particular comparison function, as in the following example.

```c
int comp_dict(const void *a, const void *b)
{
    struct Dictionary *d1 = (struct Dictionary
    *)a;  struct  Dictionary  *d2  =  (struct
    Dictionary *)b; return strcmp(d1->word, d2-
    >word);
}
```

Thus, if we were to create an array dt[100] of type struct Dictionary, we could sort it as follows.

```c
qsort(dt, NELEMS(dt), sizeof(dt[0]), comp_dict);
```

Generic code that relies on function pointers typically comes at the price of reduced efficiency due to function-call overhead. The function qsort() incurs function-call overhead for each comparison, and so tends to be less efficient than a custom-built quick-sort algorithm. In C++ the facilities of templates and inlined functions avoid these runtime penalties and permit the construction of generic code that is as efficient as custom-built code.

**Chapter 15**

## Data Structures

One of the key elements in software design is to determine which data-structures are most appropriate for the problem at hand. Data-structures determine how information is stored and exchanged, and have a significant effect on the overall cohesiveness, clarity, and efficiency of the program.

The C language provides pointers, arrays and structs as the basic facilities upon which powerful high-level data-structures may be created. (However, these data-structures are not specific to C, and may be implemented similarly in other programming languages.) In this chapter we examine several of the more common constructions, but we only scratch the surface of the great ensemble of existing data-structures. For more information, the interested reader is directed to a good algorithms and data-structures textbook. For simplicity, the implementations presented below are written for specific data-types; converting them to generic code is left as an exercise.

### 1.     Efficiency and Time Complexity

Efficiency, in terms of execution speed, can be approached at two levels. One is to optimise the execution of a set of loops and expressions in a process of *code tuning*. These are small-scale optimisations, which attempt to replace expensive operations with faster ones. The following are common examples.

- Replace array indexing with pointer operations.

- Replace power-of-two integer multiplication and division with bitwise shift operations.

- Manually unroll loops to avoid the overhead of branching and conditional expression evaluation for each iteration.

- Move non-changing expressions outside of loops to avoid unnecessary re-evaluation.

- Replace functions with macros to avoid function-call overhead.

The gains for such adjustments are typically small, and often come at the price of considerable loss of code clarity. Also, many of these optimisations are performed automatically by modern compilers. In fact, manual code tuning may actually result in *slower* execution than the original (simpler) code as the more obscure operations might be less amenable to compiler optimisation. In general, small-scale code optimisation should be avoided until proven necessary. That is, the program should be written with a focus on correctness and clarity, and subsequently tested for bottlenecks using a *profiler*. A profiler is a software tool that measures where a program spends most of its time, and enables code tuning to be focused where it is actually needed. Finally, to ensure that tuning actually has the desired effect, it is essential to measure the code segment execution time both before and after applying optimisations.

*Some programmers pay too much attention to efficiency; by worrying too soon about little "optimizations" they create ruthlessly clever programs that are insidiously difficult to maintain. Others pay too little attention; they end up with beautifully structured programs that are utterly inefficient and therefore useless. Good programmers keep efficiency in context: it is just one of many problems in software, but it is sometimes very important [Ben00, page 87].*

The second approach to efficiency concerns code organisation on a larger scale; it concerns the choice of algorithms and data-structures. These decisions tend to have a much greater effect on program speed, often by orders-of-magnitude. The central concept in this approach is the property of *time complexity*, which is a measure of how long an algorithm will take to complete given a certain size input. Time complexity is usually expressed in terms of *O-notation* which, in essence, states an upper-bound on computation to within a constant factor. For example, to search for a particular item in an unordered array of $n$ elements is a linear operation; it takes on average $O(n)$ iterations to find the item (or to show that the item is missing). Informally, *$O(n)$* may be understood as meaning "to the order n" or "linear with respect to n". Common time complexities encountered for collections of n items include constant time $O(1)$, logarithmic time $O(\log n)$, linear time $O(n)$, and quadratic time $O(n^2)$.

Aside. A third important factor with regard to efficiency is the effect of the memory hierarchy on computation speed. Registers, caches, RAM, and virtual memory all incur different access penalties, with each lower level in the hierarchy often costing several orders-of-magnitude greater runtime than its predecessor. Different algorithms and data-structures have different memory interaction behaviours, and an algorithm that involves less instructions on paper may actually run significantly slower than another. Algorithms that exploit space optimisation, locality of reference, and other memory-friendly techniques are usually much faster than those that don't. A thorough discussion of memory hierarchy issues is well beyond the scope of this text.

## 1.  **Arrays**

The simplest of all data-structures is the array. It is directly supported by the C language and defines a contiguous sequence of elements in memory. It groups together a set of variables of the same type, and permits iteration over the set. If an array is of fixed size, known at compile-time, it can be allocated on the stack, otherwise, its size may be determined at run-time and allocated on the heap via malloc(). The expandable vector (see Sections 9.5, 11.7, and 14.2.1) is a good example of an array whose size may be grown dynamically at run-time.

For an array of size n, to access or change the value of an array element is an $O(1)$ operation. However, to insert or remove an element from the middle of an array is $O(n)$, as the elements following that point must be shuffled along by one. A linear search of an array is $O(n)$; a binary search of a sorted array is $O(\log n)$.

1. **Linked Lists**

2.      A linked-list is a set of nodes, where each node contains an item of data and a pointer to the next node in the list. Linked-lists come in two basic varieties: singly linked and doubly linked. The implementation of singly linked-lists is covered in Section 11.4, and so here we will present code for a doubly linked-list.

For simplicity, let the contained item be an integer. A list node is defined as

```
typedef struct List
List; struct List {
        int item;        /* Contained item. */
        List *next;      /* Pointer to next node in list. */
        List *prev;      /* Pointer to previous node in list. */
};
```

The following functions perform node insertion and deletion operations, which may be applied at any point along the list.

```
1. struct List *insert_after(List *node, int item)
2. /* Add new item to the next position in the list after 'node'. Return pointer to new node. */
3. {
/* Allocate memory for new node. */
List *newnode = (List *) malloc(sizeof(List)); if (newnode == NULL)
        return NULL; /* allocation failed */

/* If list is not empty, splice new node into list. */ if (node) {
        newnode->next = node->next; newnode->prev = node; node->next = newnode;
        newnode->next->prev = newnode;
}
else { /* empty list, make new head node. */ newnode->next = NULL; newnode->prev = NULL;
}
newnode->item = item; return newnode;
 4
 5
 6
 7
1.   9
10 11 12
13
14
15
16
17
18
19
1.   21 22
2. }
24
1. void delete_node(List *node)
2. /* Remove node and reconnect links on either side. */
3. {
```

```
4.      if (node->prev) node->prev->next = node->next;
5.      if (node->next) node->next->prev = node->prev;
6.      free(node);
7.   }
```

10-15 Given a pointer to a node already in the list, the new node is inserted in the position immediately following. Existing links are connected to the new node to effectively splice it into the list.

16-19 However, if the node pointer passed to this function is NULL, it simply creates a new node with links in both directions pointing to NULL. That is, it creates a new list of length one.

28-30 To remove a node from a list, the nodes on either side are first connected together, and then the selected node is deleted. The if-statements check that the adjacent links were not NULL.

Insertion and removal of nodes from anywhere along a list is O(1), provided a pointer to the specified location is already available. Thus, linked-lists are a good choice if insertion/removal operations are frequent into the middle of a sequence. However, search along a list of size n is $O(n)$, and so other data-structures (such as a sorted array) are preferred if the sequence is very long and searching is a common operation.

## 1.      **Circular Buffers**

A circular buffer, like an array or linked-list, contains a sequence of elements. The difference is that this data-structure has fixed size and its end loops back to its beginning. Circular buffers are usually implemented with either an array or a linked-list as the underlying representation. (In the latter case, the end-node points back to the head-node.) In this section, we describe an array-based implementation.

The basic form of a circular buffer is shown in Figure 15.1. The buffer is allocated a fixed amount of space, and may contain no more elements than this maximum. There are two indexes into the buffer marking the front and back, respectively. The front index points to the empty slot where the next element will be added. The back index points to the next element to be extracted. Thus, items are pushed onto the front of the buffer and removed from the back. After each addition or removal, the associated index is moved forward to the next position and, when an index reaches the end of the buffer, it is cycled around to the beginning, so that the buffer appears as a continuous loop. (This continuity is represented naturally by a linked-list, with the connection of the end-node back to the head-node being no different to any other link. However, for an array-based implementation, special wrap-around operations must be performed for the end of the array.)

| | | item | item | item | | |
|---|---|---|---|---|---|---|

**back**                                **front**

Figure 15.1: Circular buffer. Items are added to the front and extracted from the back. The end of the buffer wraps around to the beginning to form a continuous loop.

Circular buffers are very common in real-time and embedded systems where there are various processes that communicate with each other. One process is a producer and puts data into the buffer, and another is a consumer and removes data from the buffer. The buffer acts as temporary storage to allow both processes to operate asynchronously, with neither process having to wait for the other to complete a transaction.

For our array-based implementation, we define the circular buffer type as follows.

```c
typedef struct CircBuf_t {
    ValueType *array;    /* Pointer to array of items. */
    int       size;      /* Maximum number of items in buffer. */
    int       nelems;    /* Current number of items in buffer. */
    int       front;     /* Index to front of buffer. */
    int       back;      /* Index to back of buffer. */
} CircBuf;
```

The public interface is exported in a header file, and provides operations to create and destroy a buffer, to add and extract items, and to get the current size and maximum size of the buffer. Notice that, once again, the structure CircBuf is an *opaque type* with its definition hidden within the private interface.

```c
1. typedef double ValueType;
2. typedef struct CircBuf_t CircBuf;
3
1. /* create-destroy buffer */
2. CircBuf *create_buffer(int size);
3. void destroy_buffer(CircBuf *cb);
7
1. /* add-remove elements */
2. int add_item(CircBuf *cb, const ValueType *item);
3. int get_item(CircBuf *cb, ValueType *item);
11
1. /* query state */
2. int get_nitems(const CircBuf *cb);
3. int get_size(const CircBuf *cb);
```

The two functions below form the crux of the buffer data-structure—insertion and extraction. Their implementation is straightforward, with the wrap-around code being the only subtlety.

```
1.  int add_item(CircBuf *cb, const ValueType *item)
2.  /* Add a new element to front of buffer.
3.   * Returns 0 for success, and -1 if buffer is full. */
4.  {
5.          if (cb->nelems == cb->size)
6.                  return -1;
7
1.          cb->array[cb->front] = *item;
2.          if (++cb->front == cb->size) /* wrap around */
3.                  cb->front = 0;
4.          ++cb->nelems;
5.          return 0;
6.  }
14
1.  int get_item(CircBuf *cb, ValueType *item)
2.  /* Remove element from back of buffer, and assign it to *item.
3.   * Returns 0 for success, and -1 if buffer is empty. */
4.  {
5.          if (cb->nelems == 0)
6.                  return -1;
21
1.          --cb->nelems;
2.          *item = cb->array[cb->back];
3.          if (++cb->back == cb->size) /* wrap around */
4.                  cb->back = 0;
5.          return 0;
6.  }
```

5-6 Check whether buffer is full. Circular buffers generally deal with being full in one of two ways. First, as in this example, they might return a flag to indicate full status. A second option is to over-write existing items so that, for a buffer of size n, only the most recent n elements are retained. That is, when the buffer is full, the front index meets the back index. If another element is inserted, *both* indexes are incremented and the back item is lost.

9-10 When the front index reaches the end of the array, it must be reset to zero to point to the beginning of the array again. A common alternative to this comparison code is the following idiom, which uses the modulus operator to bound the index.

cb->front = (cb->front + 1) % cb->size; /* wrap around */

Aside. A common difficulty with all the data-structure implementations presented in this chapter, and with algorithm design in general, is ensuring correct behaviour for *boundary conditions*. Boundary conditions occur at the extremities of normal algorithm operation. For example, the boundaries for a circular buffer occur when the buffer is full or empty, or when the indices wrap around. Care must be taken to avoid "off-by-one" indexing errors, and to make the appropriate choices of pre- or post-increment. Checking boundary conditions is an important technique for finding subtle bugs.

*The idea is that most bugs occur at boundaries. If a piece of code is going to fail, it will likely fail at a boundary. Conversely, if it works at its boundaries, its likely to work elsewhere too [KP99, page 140].*

## 1.　**Stacks**

A stack, also known as a *last-in-first-out* (LIFO) buffer, is used to store items and then extract them in reverse order. The basic form is shown in Figure 15.2. The stack grows upwards as items are pushed onto the top, and shrinks back down as items are popped off the top. Stacks with fixed maximum size are usually implemented with a simple array. If a stack does not have a fixed maximum, it might be implemented using a dynamic representation such as our expandable vector.

Figure 15.2: Stack. Items are pushed onto the top of the stack and popped off the top in reverse order.

As an example implementation, consider the following data type for a stack with maximum size MAXSIZE.

```
typedef struct Stack {
    double buffer[MAXSIZE]; /* Stack buffer. */
    int count;                /* Number of elements in stack. */
} Stack;
```

The code for pushing items onto the stack and popping them off is trivial. (We neglect bounds checking, for brevity.)

```
void push(Stack *s, double item) { s->buffer[s->count++] = item;
} double pop(Stack *s) { return s->buffer[—s->count]; }
```

## 1.　**Queues**

A queue, otherwise known as a *first-in-first-out* (FIFO) buffer, represents the other side of the coin to a stack. Where a stack pushes and pops items from the top (or front) of the buffer, a queue pushes items on at the front and pops them off at the back. Thus, a queue removes items in the same order as they were placed onto it.

The basic form of a queue is shown in Figure 15.3. If a queue has fixed maximum size, it becomes equivalent to a circular buffer. Variable length queues are a little more complicated. That is, they are difficult to implement efficiently with an expandable vector, but are well suited to implementation with a singly linked-list. Another alternative is to use a *deque,* which is a linked-list of short arrays and provides certain efficiency advantages of both arrays and lists.

The following implementation demonstrates a fixed size queue, which is a simple wrapper of the circular buffer described above. Once again, we neglect error checking for the sake of brevity, but the basic operations are clear.

```
typedef CircBuf Queue;
void push(Queue *q, ValueType item) { add_item(q, &item); }
ValueType pop(Queue *q) { ValueType v; get_item(q, &v); return v; }
```

**back**
**item**
**item**
**item**
**item**
**front**

Figure 15.3: Queue. Items are pushed onto the queue from the front and popped off from the back. Thus, items are extracted in the same order as they were inserted.

# 1. Binary Trees

**root**

**NULL    NULL**

Figure 15.4: Binary tree. The top node is the root node. Each node contains an item of data and has two links to child nodes, which may point to NULL. In this figure, the bottom and righthand nodes are leaf nodes.

Binary trees are self-referential structures like linked-lists; they consist of nodes that point to other nodes. However, where list nodes point to adjacent nodes in a linear manner, tree nodes point to *child* nodes in a branching descent structure as shown in Figure 15.4. Each node has two pointers, which point to a left and a right child node, respectively. If a particular child does not exist, the pointer is NULL, and if both pointers are NULL, the node is called a *leaf* node. The top node in the tree is called the *root* node.

Binary trees are useful for storing data in sorted order. If the data were to be stored first and sorted second, then an array or list would be the right data-structure for the job. But neither is particularly efficient for storing data in sorted order as it arrives; they both take O(n) time to insert a new item into a set that already contains n elements. For a *balanced* tree containing $n$ elements, insertion of a new node in sorted order takes O(log n) time. (A balanced tree is a tree with the minimum possible depth; it has no nodes at a level lower than the highest NULL branch. Figure 15.4 is a balanced tree.) Furthermore, a balanced tree permits O(logn) search for items, and the entire tree may be examined in sorted order in $O(n)$ operations.

The following implementation presents a binary tree that contains two items of ancillary data: a string and an integer. This structure, and the associated functions, are used to implement a wordcounting algorithm similar to that presented in [KR88, pages 139-143]. From this example, more generic use of binary trees should be apparent. The Tree structure contains the two data items and pointers to left and right Tree nodes as follows.

```
struct Tree {
    char *item;        /* Contained string. */
    int count;         /* Count of string appearances. */
    Tree *left;        /* Pointer to left-child. */
    Tree *right;       /* Pointer to right-child. */
```

The module's public interface exports the name of the Tree data-type and four functions to manipulate the tree. These perform operations to add new strings, count the occurrences of a specified string, print all strings in lexicographic order, and delete the entire tree structure, respectively.

1. typedef struct Tree Tree;

1. Tree *add_item(Tree *root, const char *item);
2. int count_item(Tree *root, const char *item);
3. void print_inorder(Tree *root);
4. void destroy_tree(Tree *root);

The function below is the implementation for adding a new string to the tree. Its basic operation is to first search for whether the word already exists in the tree. If so, it increments the count for that word. Otherwise, it adds the new word to the tree with a count of one. Trees (and linked-lists also), being self-referential structures, are well suited to recursive algorithms, and this is the case here: add_item() calls itself recursively until either the word is found, or an empty space is located in which to store a new word.

```
1.  Tree *add_item(Tree *node, const char *item)
2.  /* Search for whether item already exists in tree. If not, add it to first empty
3.   * node location (in lexicographical order), if found, increment word count. Perform,
4.   * recursive descent for search, return pointer to current node. */
5.  {
6.      int cmp;
7.
1.      if (node == NULL) /* found empty tree location, add item */
2.          return make_node(item);
10.
1.      /* Recursive comparison to put item in correct location. */
2.      cmp = strcmp(item, node->item);
3.      if (cmp < 0)
4.          node->left = add_item(node->left, item);
5.      else if (cmp > 0)
6.          node->right = add_item(node->right, item);
7.      else
8.          ++node->count; /* item already in tree, increment count */
19.
1.      return node;
2.  }
```

8-9 If the passed pointer is NULL, a new node is created by calling make_node() and a pointer to this node is returned. The make_node() function is part of the module's private interface; it allocates memory for the new node, and initialises it with a copy of the passed string and a count of one.

12 The binary tree stores words in lexicographic order. This ordering is accomplished using strcmp() to determine whether a word is less than, greater than, or equal to the word contained by the current node.

13-14 If the word is less than the node word, we recurse using the node's left-hand child. Notice how the return value of add_item() is used to connect lower-level nodes with their parent nodes.

15-16 If the word is greater than the node word, we recurse using the node's right-hand child.

17-18 If the words are equal (i.e., a match has been found), the count for that node is incremented and the recursive search terminates.

There are three points to note from this function. The first is that the recursive search terminates when either a word match is found (lines 17 and 18) or we reach a NULL node (lines 8 and 9) indicating that we have a new word. Second, when a new child node is created, it is attached to its parent node via the return value (lines 9, 14 and 16). And third, the recursion, as it splits to the left and right, orders insertion and search, giving the tree its O(log n) properties.

The next two functions perform binary search and in-order visitation, respectively. The first, count_item() searches the tree for a word match, and returns the word count if a match is found, and zero if it is not. (The word count is the number of times a particular word was sent to add_item().) This function demonstrates an iterative (i.e., non-recursive) method for traversing the tree. The second function, print_inorder() visits every node in the tree and prints the stored word and word count. (The function print_node() is part of the module's private interface.) The recursive implementation of print_inorder() causes the nodes to be printed in sorted order.

```c
int count_item(Tree *root, const char *item)
/* Search for item in tree and return its count. */
{
        while (root) {
                int cmp =
                strcmp(item, root-
                >item); if (cmp < 0)
                        root =
                root->left;
                else if (cmp >
                0)
                        root = root-> right;
                else
                        return root->count;
        }
        return 0;
}

void print_inorder(Tree *node)
/* Print tree in lexicographical order */
{
        if (node ==
        NULL) return;
        print_inorder(n
        ode->left);
        print_node(nod
        e);
        print_inorder(n
        ode->right);
}
```

The basic binary tree, as presented here, is sufficient for a great many situations. It is well suited to problems where the data arrives in random order, such as the words from a book. However, it behaves very inefficiently if the data does not arrive in random order and the tree becomes unbalanced. In the worst case, if the data is added to the tree in sorted order, the tree obtains the appearance and properties of a linked-list, with insert and search times being O(n).

Various solutions exist that resolve this problem. Advanced binary tree implementations, such as *red-black trees*, remain balanced for any input. Also, a data-structure called a *skip list*, while entirely different to a binary tree, possesses the same insertion and search properties as for a balanced binary tree.

Finally, even when the data is suitable for a simple binary tree implementation, it might not be the best data-structure for the job. Trees are best suited to tasks where the data is to be in sorted order *during* the insertion phase. However, if the data is to be stored in any order, and fast search is required *subsequently*, it is usually more efficient to store the data in an (expandable) array and then sort the array. With a good sorting algorithm, the time required to sort an array is less than the time to insert data into a tree. Similarly, the time to perform a binary search of a sorted array is generally less than the time to search a tree. Also, arrays consume less space than trees. The key advice here is to be aware of the tradeoffs between data-structures, and know when one is likely to be more suitable than another.

## 1.    Hash Tables

A hash table is a data-structure that uses a *hash function* to compute an index into an array. The most common form of hash table, and the easiest to explain, is one that combines an array of pointers with a set of linked-lists. The basic form of this type of hash table is shown in Figure 15.5. Each pointer in the array of pointers points to the head of a singly linked-list. A list may be empty, in which case the pointer is NULL. Each element in the array is called a "bucket", and the list pointed to by a bucket is called a "chain".

Figure 15.5: Hash table. An array of pointers (buckets) point to singly linked-lists (chains). A hash function converts an item value into a bucket index, which restricts search to the attached chain. Each chain may be zero length or greater.

The operation of a hash table is as follows. Given an item of data to be stored in the table, the hash function computes an index based on the value of this item. The index is such that it falls within the bounds of the pointer array, and so specifies one of the buckets. The selected bucket points to a linked-list, which is searched to check whether the item is already stored, otherwise the item is added to the front of the list.

The key to an efficient hash table is a good hash function. Essentially it should distribute items evenly between the different buckets and not favour any particular bucket over another. The derivation of hash functions involves fairly advanced mathematics including aspects of probability theory and prime number theory. Also, the length of the array of pointers should not be arbitrary but itself a prime number. We will not discuss these issues further as they are beyond the scope of this text.

A hash table is useful for implementing very fast lookup tables. The hash function computes a bucket index in $O(1)$ time and, assuming the chain is short, the linear link-list search is very quick. Provided the hash function distributes items evenly, the chains will be short enough so that the entire operation may be considered $O(1)$. Thus, on average, hash tables permit $O(1)$ lookup, although in the worst case, where the hash function places all items in a single bucket, lookup can be $O(n)$.

In the following example we use a hash table to implement a dictionary. The dictionary is built up of words and their associated definitions. These word-definition pairs are stored in the hash table using the word as a search key. The hash table permits fast insertion, search and deletion, and the public interface for this module is shown below.

1. typedef struct Dictionary_t Dictionary;
2
1. Dictionary *create_table(void);
2. void destroy_table(Dictionary *);
5
1. int add_word(Dictionary *, const char *key, const char *defn);
2. char *find_word(const Dictionary *, const char *key);
3. void delete_word(Dictionary *, const char *key);

   The next section of code shows part of the private interface. The #define (line 1) specifies the size of the array of pointers (i.e., the number of buckets). Notice this value is prime. Lines 3 to 7 define the link-list node type. Each node in a chain contains a word, its definition, and a pointer to the next node. The Dictionary type (lines 9 to 11) contains an array of pointers to the chain nodes; this is the array of buckets. The hash function (lines 13 to 22) is a complicated device, and we will not elaborate on its workings here. It was obtained from [KR88, page 144], and to quote this text, it "is not the best possible hash function, but it is short and effective." Notice that it takes a string argument and converts it to a bucket index.

```
#define
HASHSIZE

101 struct

Nlist {
        char  word;               /* search word */
        char *defn;               /* word definition */
        struct Nlist *next; /* pointer to next entry in chain */
};

struct Dictionary_t {
        struct Nlist *table[HASHSIZE]; /* table is an array of pointers to entries */
};

static unsigned hash_function(const char *str)
/* Hashing function converts a string to an index within hash table. */
{
        const int
        HashValue =
        31; unsigned
        h;

        for (h = 0; *str !=
        '\0'; ++str) h = *str
        + HashValue * h;
        return h %
        HASHSIZE;
}
```

   The two functions that follow demonstrate the main workings of the hash table algorithm. The first, and most instructive, is add_word(), which takes a word-definition pair and adds it to the table. If the word is already stored, the old definition is replaced with the new one, otherwise, if the word is not found, a new table entry is added. The second function, find_word(), uses the same search mechanism as add_word() to determine if a word is stored in the table and, if so,

returns the associated definition.
```
1.                 diet->table[i] = pnode;
2.         }
3.         return  0;
4. }
```
29
```
1.  char *find_word (const Dictionary *dict, const char *key)
2.  /* Find definition for keyword. Return NULL if key not found. */
3.  {
4.         unsigned i = hash_function(key); /* get table index */
5.         struct  Nlist      *pnode = dict->table[i];
```
35
```
1.         while (pnode && strcmp(pnode->word, key) != 0) /* search index chain */
2.             pnode = pnode—>next;
```
38
```
1.         if (pnode) /* match found */
2.             return pnode—>defn;
3.         return  NULL;
4. }
```

5-6 The word is passed to the hash function, which computes an array index. This bucket, in turn, points to the head of a node chain.

8-9 We search the length of the chain looking for a string match between the keyword and a node word.

11-18 If the node pointer is not NULL then a match was found before the end of the chain. Thus, we replace the old definition with the new one. (Note, the function allocate_string() is part of the module's private interface and makes a duplicate of the passed string.)

19-26 If the end of the chain was reached, then the keyword is new and is added to the head of the chain. (Note, the function makenode() is part of the module's private interface; it creates and initialises a Nlist node.)

33-37 This code is identical to lines 5 to 9 in add_word().

39-41 If the keyword is found, return a pointer to its definition, otherwise return NULL.

The above example demonstrates a specific hash table implementation for storing a specific type of data (i.e., strings). Writing a generic version of a hash table is not trivial because different data types typically require different hash functions. However, a generic implementation is possible by using a function pointer to permit user-supplied hash functions. (A default hash function might be called if the user passes NULL.)

As always, deciding whether a hash table is the right data-structure for a particular problem is a matter of considering tradeoffs. Hash tables provide very fast O(1) add, delete, and find operations on average, if supplied with an effective hash function. However, they can have bad O(n) worst-case behaviour, and in some circumstances the O(log n) worst-case complexity of a balanced tree (e.g., a red-black tree) might be preferred.

# Chapter 16

## C in the Real World

This text has covered most of the core ISO C language and its use. However, virtually all useful software systems make use of some form to extension to standard C. This chapter provides a sampling of the virtually limitless field of extensions and related topics with regard to writing C programs in the real world. Knowledge of the core language is the foundation upon which all these additional topics rely.

TODO: complete this chapter...

### 1.      **Further ISO C Topics**

There are many details of ISO C and the standard library that are not covered in this text. For the most part, these topics are peripheral, and do not impinge on the majority of application programming. They include:

- Complete rules of operator precedence and order of evaluation.
- Keywords such as register and volatile.
- Memory alignment and padding.
- Changes to the standard with ISO C99. For the most part, this standard to backward compatible with C89, and the older standard currently remains the more important language in practice.

One topic that is fundamental but cannot be adequately covered in this book is the standard library; the majority of standard functions are not even mentioned. These functions are frequently useful and are worthy of study. They include, input and output (stdio.h), mathematical functions (math.h), strings (string.h), utilities (stdlib.h), time (time.h), floating-point specifications (float.h), errors (errno.h), assertions (assert.h), variable-length argument lists (stdarg.h), signal handling (signal.h), non-local jumps (setjmp.h), etc.

For more on these and other topics, consult a good reference textbook. A complete and authoritative reference is [HS95, HS02], and is highly recommended for practicing programmers. An excellent FAQ [Sum95] on the C language discusses many of the more difficult aspects. It is worth noting that many C idioms are not recorded in any textbook and can only be discovered from practical experience and reading the source code of others.

Note. Different compilers may conform to the standard to different extent. They might not permit conforming code to compile, or it might exhibit non-standard behaviour. This is less likely with modern compilers. More likely is allowing non-standard code to compile. As a rule, it is wise to compile code on several different compilers to ensure standard conformance.

### 1.      **Traditional C**

The C language was created in the early 1970s and, over the next decade or so, grew and evolved substantially, until finally being standardised in 1989. Prior to 1989, the original language reference was defined by the first edition of *The C Programming Language* by Kernighan and Ritchie in 1978. This version is now called "classic C" or "K&R C", and has significant differences to ISO C. The most noticeable difference is that functions did not have prototypes, and a function definition that we would now write as

```
double func(int a, int b, char c)
{

}
```

would be written as

```
double func(a, b, c) int a, b;
char c;
{

}
```

Standard C, with the introduction of prototypes, provides far stronger type-checking than was previously available.

## 1.    **Make Files**

Make-files manage the organisation of a C program, which may consist of numerous source and header files and possibly other precompiled libraries. Makefiles manage compilation dependencies and linking, and permit partial compilation, so that only those parts of the program that have changed need to be recompiled. Makefiles can be complicated, and a simple example would be of limited value. They are platform dependent, and some compiler environments (e.g., Microsoft Visual Studio) manage project Makefiles automatically via the IDE. For more information, consult a textbook or read existing makefiles.

Two examples worth examining are GNU-Make (GMAKE) and CMAKE. The first is ...

TODO - add reference to GMAKE - add reference to CMAKE - cross-platform makefile generation

## 1.    **Beyond the C Standard Library**

The standard C language provides the foundation on which ...
- but is limited in the capabilities of the standard library.
- API *(application programming interface)*
- standard APIs: POSIX - platforms: Win32 API, etc - Non-standard extensions. Graphics (OpenGL, VTK), GUI frameworks, threads, interrupts, real-time, hardware, audio, serial comms, sockets, file-structure—directories.
- to write portable code, isolate non-portable parts in modules in separate files and write wrapper interfaces, then to port just need to write a few platform specific internals.

## 1.    **Interfacing With Libraries**

- many open-source C libraries - other repositories: - source forge - planet source code - www.program.com/source
- linux?? - netlib

- Separate ISO C conforming code from proprietry or platform specific - Interface with precompiled libraries, open-source libraries, - discuss libraries as an example of modular design.


1. **Mixed Language Programming**

There arise situations where a C program must call a set of routines written in another programming language, such as assember, C++, FORTRAN, Matlab, etc.
- Interfacing C with FORTRAN, assembler, C++, MatLab, etc. - binding


1. **Memory Interactions**

Historically, instruction count was a premium. Computer processors were slow and memory was tiny, and the speed of an algorithm was directly proportional to the number of instructions it required. Programmers spent a lot of effort finding ways to minimise instruction count. Most algorithm textbooks today continue to use this measure in their analysis of algorithm complexity.

Modern computers, with fast CPUs, are no longer constrained primarily by instruction execution.

Today, the bottleneck is memory access. While ever waiting for instructions or data to be fetched from memory, the CPU is idle and cycles are wasted. To minimise idle time, modern computer architectures employ a *memory hierarchy,* a set of memory levels of different size and speed to permit faster access to frequently used information. This hierarchy, from fastest to slowest, consists of registers, cache, main random access memory (RAM), hard-disk, and magnetic tape. Very fast memory is small and expensive, while cheap large-scale memory, such as RAM, is relatively slow.

Each level in the hierarchy is typically slower than the level above by several orders-of-magnitude. Information is transferred up and down the memory hierarchy automatically by the operating system, with the exception of magnetic tape, which is usually reserved for memory backup. Essentially all modern operating systems manage the transfer of data between RAM and hard-disk, so that the hard-disk appears as additional, albeit slow, RAM known as *virtual memory.*

As the CPU accesses instructions or data, the required information is transferred up the hierarchy.

If the information is already in registers, it can be executed immediately. If it resides in cache, it is moved up to the registers and the old register data is transferred back to cache. Similarly "lines" of RAM are moved up into cache, and "pages" of hard-disk memory are moved up to RAM. Since the amount of information that can be stored in the upper levels is limited, data that has not been accessed recently is passed back down to lower levels. For example, if all cache lines are full and a new line is required from RAM, the *least recently used* cache line is returned to RAM.

Information is transferred between levels in blocks, so that when a particular item is accessed, it brings with it a neighbourhood of instructions or data. Thus, if the next item required was a neighbour, that item is already in cache and is available for immediate execution. This property is called *"locality of reference"* and has significant influence on algorithm speed. An algorithm with a large instruction count but good locality may perform much faster than another algorithm with smaller instruction count. Some algorithms that look fast on paper are slow in practice due to bad cache interaction.

There are various factors that affect locality of reference. One is program size. There is usually a tradeoff between size and speed, whereby to use less memory the program requires the execution of more instructions and vice-versa. However, a program that is optimised for size, that attempts to occupy minimal space, may also achieve better speed as it is better able to fit within cache lines. Another factor is data-structures. Some data-structures such as link-lists may develop bad locality if naively implemented, whereas others, such as arrays, possess very good locality. A third factor is the way an algorithm utilises a data-structure. For example, in numerical computing, matrix multiplication can be sped up by orders-of-magnitude by using "blocking" algorithms, which operate over sub-matrix blocks rather than over an entire large matrix.

The use of dynamic memory—allocation from the heap—can significantly affect program execution speed. Access to operating system resources, such as dynamic memory and input-output, is generally slow and should be minimised as a rule. (Functions like printf() manage this automatically by buffering characters and only sending them to the OS when the buffer is full or when explicitly flushed.) Allocating many small objects on the heap is very inefficient, in time and space, as each allocation involves a search for space and bookkeeping records. Also, over successive allocations and deallocations, the heap tends to become fragmented and develops bad locality-of- reference. Heap allocation becomes even slower in multi-threaded environments, as each allocation involves locking and unlocking operations for thread synchronisation.

One approach to alleviating heap allocation overhead is to use *arenas*. An arena is a data- structure that wraps the global memory allocator and allocates an internal cache of memory in large chunks. Clients use the arena to perform local allocations, and obtain portions of the arena cache. Arenas possess several advantages: They can avoid the space overhead of general-purpose allocator records, they avoid the time overhead of thread-safe allocation, and they prevent memory leaks by providing centralised deallocation.

1.      **Advanced Algorithms and Data Structures**

The data structures presented in Chapter 15 represent arguably the most common and useful constructs for most programs. However, there exist a vast number of more sophisticated data structures for more specialised problems. Examples include red-black binary trees, B-trees, graphs, finite state machines, etc.

The literature on advanced algorithms is also vast. On the topic of sorting alone, there are many variations of Quicksort that alleviate its $O(n^2)$ worst-case behaviour. There are also special-case sorting algorithms that have linear-time complexity for problems with appropriate structure. Other forms of algorithms include searching, selection, numerical computation, etc. For further reading, the following texts are recommended [Sed98, CLRS01, Knu98a, PTVF92].